JUL 04

THE
HELLFIGHTERS
of HARLEM

Some Other Books by Bill Harris

One Thousand New York Buildings
The World Trade Center: A Tribute
Black and White New York
A History of New York City
America's Medal of Honor
Israel: The Promised Land
Lost Civilizations
Sidewalks of New York
The Plaza Hotel
New York at Night
New York: An Anthology (editor)
New York: City of Many Dreams
New York: A Photographic Journey
New York from the Air
Long Island
An American Moment
Spirit of the South

THE
HELLFIGHTERS
of HARLEM

African-American Soldiers Who
Fought for the Right
to Fight for Their Country

BILL HARRIS

CARROLL & GRAF PUBLISHERS
NEW YORK

THE HELLFIGHTERS OF HARLEM
*African-American Soldiers Who Fought for the Right
to Fight for Their Country*

Carroll & Graf Publishers
An Imprint of Avalon Publishing Group Inc.
161 William Street, 16th Floor
New York, NY 10038

Copyright © 2002 by Bill Harris

First Carroll & Graf edition 2002

All photographs are used by permission of the National Archive
in Washington, D.C.

Library of Congress Cataloging-in-Publication Data is available.

ISBN: 0-7867-1050-0

Printed in the United States of America
Distributed by Publishers Group West

CONTENTS

THE HELLFIGHTERS
of HARLEM

PROLOGUE: WHY DO WE MARCH?

The beat of muffled drums was the only sound that was heard on Fifth Avenue in New York on that steamy summer Saturday afternoon, July 28, 1917. Six thousand men, women and children were marching there, from 59th down to 23rd Street, and another twenty thousand lined the sidewalks to show support for them. Yet the slow cadence of the drums was all that could be heard.

In a way, this was a funeral march. More than two hundred African-Americans had been slaughtered in the worst race riot in American history at East St. Louis, Illinois, three weeks earlier, and there had been lynchings and other atrocities at Waco, Texas and Memphis, Tennessee since then.

But the march in New York was also a silent protest against racism in America, organized by the National Association for the Advancement of Colored People, and led by writers William Edward Burghardt Du Bois and James Weldon Johnson, who had been among the founders of the NAACP six years earlier.

Their banners spoke for them. "We Are Maligned and Murdered Where We Work," said one. "Cain, Where Is Thy Brother, Abel?" asked another. And a third pointed out: "India Is Abolishing Caste. America Is Adopting It." One banner that was confiscated by the police as too inflammatory had a picture of President Woodrow Wilson with a black woman kneeling at his feet. In a reference to World War I, which the United States had just entered, it pleaded, "Bring Democracy to America Before You Take It to Europe."

The *New York Times* reported that the demonstration had been by ". . . a people of one race, united by ties of blood and color, and working for a common cause." Flyers that were distributed along the parade route described that common cause under the heading, "Why Do We March?"

"We march because by the grace of God and the force of truth, the dangerous hampering walls of prejudice and inhuman injustices must fall." It went on to call for making it impossible to repeat the recent race riots by arousing the country's consciousness and bringing the murderers to justice. It declared "total opposition [to] the hosts of evils that are forced upon us," and it concluded by saying, "We march because we want our children to live in a better land and enjoy fairer conditions than have fallen our lot."

But the message went largely unnoticed. Not long afterward, when New York's famous "Fighting 69th," the so-called Rainbow Division, marched down Fifth Avenue on its way to fight in the war in France, the 369th Colored Infantry Regiment (then known as the 15th, and, as part of the National Guard, was technically a part of New York's own) was forbidden to join them. "Black is not a color of the rainbow," was the reason given by one of its officers.

The 369th proved that black was a color of bravery, though, and as close to expressing patriotism as red, white, and blue. And after they came home, W. E. B. Du Bois wrote: "Make way for democracy. We saved it in France, and by the Great Jehovah, we will save it in the United States of America or know the reason why. We return. We return from fighting, We return fighting."

Part 1
The Pride of Harlem

The Return from Fighting

New York City loves a parade, and there have been hundreds of them, especially on Fifth Avenue, over the years. But there has never been one that involved such an outpouring of pride as the welcome New York gave to its 369th Regiment on February 17, 1919.

It was a bitter cold February day when the Harlem Hellfighters came home from the war. But although they weren't scheduled to step off on their triumphal march up Fifth Avenue until 11:30, the reviewing stand at 60th Street was filled up before 9:00 that morning by ticket-holding mothers, wives, and children of the conquering heroes. The word of the day was, "Be there and be there early."

The first arrivals walked across 59th Street from the San Juan Hill neighborhood on the west side of Broadway, where many black families still hadn't made the decision to move on up to Harlem. That neighborhood, New York's black ghetto in the last years of the nineteenth century, took its name from Theodore Roosevelt's charge up San Juan Hill in Cuba, when another group of Negro war veterans had distinguished themselves in the Spanish-American War.

Many black families had made the move up to Harlem by then, and those who had came downtown, or in from Brooklyn, in taxis or in their own cars to celebrate the great day. Some came in horse-drawn carriages, which were still common in the city in 1919. One family arrived in a plumber's wagon. In describing its occupants, the *New York World* reported: "[I]ts women members [were] all bundled up in shawls and blankets against the cold, but grinning delightedly as the whole stand applauded." Shawls and blankets were the uniform of the day among the women in the stands, too. This was their day, and they wanted to enjoy every last minute of it, no matter how cold it was.

By the time Governor Al Smith and other state and city officials finally showed up to take their places in the reviewing stand, there was hardly enough room for them. The crowd greeted them with a very loud rendition of Irving Berlin's hit song, "Oh, How I Hate to Get Up in the Morning."

At that moment, the parade itself was just getting under way at 23rd Street almost two miles downtown. In the vanguard was four platoons of mounted police riding their horses twelve abreast. Right behind them was Colonel William Hayward, who had organized the regiment back in 1913 and drilled them into the fighting machine they had become. Hayward had been wounded in the ankle during the last days of the war, but he left his crutches behind because, as he put it, "I wasn't going to peg along on the proudest day of my life."

Behind the colonel came his staff, followed by the Police Department Band. Then came the main event: the men of the 369th, almost three thousand strong. They marched twenty abreast in the tight formation preferred by the French soldiers who had been their brothers in battle. They wore helmets that had become battered in those battles, and the bayonets on their shouldered rifles gleamed in the sun. As the *Times* put it: "[T]hey made a spectacle that might justify pity for the Germans."

The newspaper went on: "On the average, this regiment is made up of big men. With their overcoats, trench hats, and bayonet-tipped guns, the impression of their bigness was heightened, and whole platoons seemed to be made up of men seven feet and over. Most of them were grim visaged from force of habit when marching or at attention, and their helmet chin straps added a hardening touch, so New York got a pretty fair idea of how they had impressed the Germans." Each of the men wore two gold stripes on one sleeve, signifying a year of combat service—almost unique among American troops, who hadn't joined the fight until it was nearly finished over there. Many of them—too many, it seemed—had stripes on the opposite sleeve, representing wounds they had suffered in battle.

Colonel Hayward called his men "those scrapping babies of mine," but it was clear that nobody else would even think of calling any of these guys "babies." There were, however, literally hundreds of babies along the line of march and in the reviewing stand. Some of these were what Hayward called "our posthumous children," whose fathers weren't coming back on this day or any other. Most, though, had been brought out to see—and be seen by—their fathers for the first time.

By the time the procession reached the 60th Street reviewing stand, the roar of the crowd, estimated at more than 250,000, might easily have been heard all the way up in Harlem. But just then it got even louder. The soldiers were marching at a quick pace, and it took only about seventeen minutes for the entire parade to pass the dignitaries and their families It was hardly enough time for any of the soldiers to do much more than smile as they rushed past their wives holding up babies for their approval.

The troops were followed by a pair of flag bearers who carried the American flag and the blue regimental standard decorated with a green and red ribbon that had a bronze medal attached to it. It was the Croix de Guerre, France's highest military honor. It had been awarded to the entire unit.

Right behind the flags, riding in an open car, was Sergeant Henry Johnson, who had earned the medal on his own. It was the high point of the parade, with shouts of "Oh, you wick-ed Henn-nery Johnson!" and "Oh, you black death!" every few feet. Johnson stood in the back of the car, with a bouquet of lilies, a gift from an admirer, in one hand, and his helmet in the other, bowing ("like a French dancemaster," said one eyewitness) and grinning broadly to the crowd during the whole seven-mile trip up to Harlem.

When he finally stepped out of his car at the end of the march, a friend pointed to the bouquet of lilies he was carrying and said, "Looks like a funeral, Henry."

The hero shot back, "Funeral for them bush Germans, boy! Sure, a funeral for them bushes!" Throughout the war, most Frenchmen called the German enemy the "boche," but Johnson and his buddies turned that into "bush," a reference to minor-league baseball teams, called the bush leagues, and usually regarded as inept. They usually added the word "Germans," so as not to offend any ballplayers.

As they paraded up the avenue, Johnson's car was followed by a fleet of ambulances carrying the nearly two hundred Hellfighters whose wounds made the long march out of the question. But the parade was far from over.

The pièce de résistance was the regiment's band that brought up the rear. The *World* described them as "One hundred strong, and the proudest band of blowers and pounders that ever reeled off marching melody."

Among their instruments was a drum that was captured from the German enemy, and five kettledrums that had been a gift of the

French government. James Reese Europe, their leader, marched at the head of the band in the full uniform of an officer (he was the regiment's highest-ranking black officer) complete with a sidearm. He had what was described as "walking pneumonia" that day, but he didn't let that stop him. His musicians wouldn't be stopped, either, no matter how exhausted they might have been.

The 369th had come back to New York aboard the French superliner SS *France* a week earlier and the Hellfighters were sent out to Camp Upton at Yaphank on Long Island, a camp some of its men had built. They rode the Long Island Rail Road into the city for their triumph, and the band started to play as soon as the train left the station at six in the morning. They never took a break all day long.

The music they played was all military marches until they crossed 110th Street and marched on up Lenox Avenue. They were finally home in Harlem, and the band changed the beat to jazz when it struck up a tune called "Here Comes My Daddy," and the syncopated rhythm didn't stop for the rest of the afternoon. The problem was that they had trouble hearing themselves above the roar of the crowd, and the crowd itself couldn't hear the music above its own din.

Every fire escape, every rooftop, every window, every sidewalk along Lenox Avenue was jam-packed with cheering humanity. Many of them were waving American flags, and nearly all of them carried flags emblazoned with the 369th's emblem, a rattlesnake coiled and ready to strike. The coiled snake appeared in shop windows, on banners, and on lapel buttons that it semed every Harlemite was wearing. Young boys showed up in army uniforms with the rattlesnake patch on their shoulders, and many of the women also wore military coats or hats decorated with the regiment's symbol.

The people in the buildings showered flowers down on the troops, but the men still didn't break ranks. They kept their cool, just as they had all the way up Fifth Avenue where they had been showered with candy, cigarettes, and silver coins nearly every step of the way.

There was another reviewing stand up at 130th Street, and Governor Smith and the other officials had gone up there for a second look, along with the Police Band, from their perch at 60th Street. But nobody was looking at them, or even making an attempt to hear their band.

The Police Department had anticipated that there would be a mob scene in Harlem when the doughboys got there, and they stationed hundreds of officers along the avenue to control it. But they weren't ready for what happened when the marchers reached home. It was pandemonium.

They had been given a preview along Central Park, when hundreds of wives and mothers ran out into Fifth Avenue to press flowers into soldiers' hands and to begin marching arm in arm with them. Colonel Hayward halted the march and ordered the women back to the sidewalks. This was a military parade, after all. But he couldn't stop the cheering. And at the end of the march, neither he nor the police could hold back the crowds. The noise was so loud that the colonel's orders couldn't be heard, and neither could the music of the regimental band. Still, Hayward kept shouting orders, and the band played on.

Finally Hayward got his men organized and ready for the next stage of the celebration. It would begin with a subway ride. The regiment was to be honored with a dinner reception downtown at the 71st Regiment Armory on Fourth Avenue (now Park Avenue South) at 34th Street, and the subway was the best way to get them there. Once they arived downtown, they were met by another wildly cheering crowd, so great that 34th Street had to be closed off for two blocks in either direction. As the men filed up the subway stairs, their families and friends were allowed though the police lines. For many of them, it was the first time that they were able to hug their own personal heroes.

There were more than 3,000 Harlemites in the galleries inside the armory, and when the boys came in, there was a crush to get down to the drill floor. It became so packed that these heroes, who had just marched seven miles, had to eat their dinner standing up. Some didn't bother eating at all. They were satisfied to sit on the sidelines among their stacked rifles with their arms around their mothers, their wives, or their girlfriends. The members of the band skipped the meal, too. Most of them stretched out in a corner of the now-deserted galleries and got a little shut-eye. By then, they had been playing nonstop for nearly twelve hours, and they had a long train ride ahead of them back out to Camp Upton, on Long Island, where they all would become civilians again the following day.

During the reception, Colonel Hayward stood up to offer a tribute to his men. But there was so much noise in the armory that nobody could hear what he had to say. If he had yelled "Fire!" at that point, nobody would have noticed. Fortunately, he held a document in his hand that said it all. It had been written by Nicholas Murray Butler, the president of Columbia University, on behalf of the people of Harlem:

> The residents of Harlem from which the 369th Infantry was so largely recruited wish to give a special and heartfelt greeting to Colonel Hayward and the officers and men of the old Fighting 15th who have made so fine a record for patriotism and courage on the soil of France.
> No American soldiers saw harder or more constant fighting and none gave a better account of themselves, whether in the Champagne, at Chateau Thierry, at the Saint Mihiel salient or in the Argonne. When fighting was to be done, the regiment was there. Two governments have given this regiment special citations for bravery in action, and among the officers and men are many who have won for themselves exceptional distinction in the service of their country.

In the rare moments he could be heard, Colonel Hayward said, "There are no better soldiers than the men of the 369th, and no soldiers have ever gotten a bigger reception in their home town."

What neither tribute mentioned, although everyone knew, was that these American soldiers had been denied the right to serve in units of their own country's army, and had fought among French troops.

At the end of this very noisy day, though, no one anywhere in the City of New York thought of the Hellfighters of Harlem as anything less than all-American boys. These men were their heroes and they were shouting it from the housetops. Other troops would come home over the next couple of weeks, and they'd all get heroes' welcomes. But none would be as exciting as the day the Hellfighters returned from fighting.

For many of them, though, the fight had only just begun.

2
PRELUDE TO WAR

Race riots, lynchings and other "incidents" were an epidemic in America during the early years of the twentieth century. Among them, the episode that made blacks think twice about serving their country took place in Houston, Texas in August 1917.

America had declared war on Germany in the spring, and as part of its buildup, the War Department established two training bases, Camp Logan and Ellington Field, at the edge of Houston. The Illinois National Guard, which included the all-black Eighth Regiment, was sent to Logan for combat training. Although most of the men of the Eighth were from the Chicago area, many of them had grown up in the South and they knew what to expect, as well as what was expected of them. Most of them resented the oppressive local segregation policies that restricted their movements every time they went into town.

The problem came to a head when the local police arrested a black soldier for interfering with their arrest of a black woman. When military policemen from the camp arrived on the scene, one of them was hit on the head, and as the other MPs ran for their lives, the local police fired at them. One MP took cover in an abandoned house, but when the rest arrived back at the base without him, a rumor spread through Camp Logan that he had been killed by the Houston police.

That was the first rumor. There would be others. As often happens, they would become self-fulfilling prophecies.

When the company commander heard a rumor that some of his men were planning to march on the local police station, he confiscated all of the rifles in the camp and detailed some men to search for loose ammunition. While the search was going on, someone shouted that a white mob was coming down the street. The troops broke into the supply tents, grabbed rifles, and started firing wildly in the general direction of what turned out to be a nonexistent mob.

Then they became a mob themselves. About one hundred of them marched off to take the fight into Houston itself. On their way, they shot and killed sixteen whites, including five police officers; four of their own men were killed as well, two of them by their own buddies. As darkness fell, they all slipped back into the camp, where their leader, Sergeant Vida Henry, shot himself in the head.

By dawn, the city had been placed under a strict curfew, and two days later the army shipped all of the black soldiers off to New Mexico. In the courts martial that followed, 110 of the 119 men accused of inciting the riot were found guilty. Two white officers among them were pardoned, but of the black soldiers, 19 were hanged, and the rest were sent to prison for the rest of their lives. All because of a series of false rumors.

Rumors spread through the North. The consensus was that the Houston riot had been a direct result of the South's "Jim Crow" laws, and that the blame rested squarely at the feet of the military for having sent black soldiers to a place like Houston to begin with.

Nearly all of the Southern states agreed that sending blacks into their midst was a big mistake, and most of them dispatched delegations to Washington to protest the practice. South Carolina even sent its governor. Several Northern states also expressed the fear that if large numbers of black troops were sent to their local military camps, they would be a menace to the surrounding populations. The War Department simply ignored all of the pleas. Black troops were sent to training camps all over the country, even though they were clearly not welcome in most localities.

Every state below the Mason-Dixon line, and some communities above it, had Jim Crow laws on their books until the 1960s. These regulations set aside separate facilities for whites and blacks, from drinking fountains to restaurants, stores, and streetcar seats. Blacks were forbidden to use "White Only" facilities, under threats of penalties that often included imprisonment. These local laws applied to military personnel as well as to civilians.

Meanwhile, up North, a great many black leaders were beginning to suggest that their brothers ought to sit out this war. They said that, considering their status in most of America, sending black soldiers into combat to defend "the American Way" would be a mockery. Asa Philip Randolph's magazine, *The Messenger*, called for "total abstinence." The Boston *Guardian,* a newspaper published for the local black community, said: "We believe in democracy, but we hold that this nation should enter the lists with clean hands," and demanded that no black man should put on a uniform until the government first renounced all forms of racism.

Other black leaders agreed that the time to end racism had come, but they argued that in the interest of patriotism, black men should answer the call and, by doing so, they would prove their loyalty and bravery. The cause of ending segregation could wait, they said. In fact, most of the cooler heads among them suggested that a good war record on the part of black troops would advance the cause far more than any strike ever would.

At the time war was declared, there were about 20,000 black men in army uniforms, trained, equipped and ready to enter the fight. Among them were the 2,053 soldiers of the 15th New York Infantry.

The unit had been formed as a National Guard regiment in 1913, as part of a long-range War Department plan to eventually form the army's 93rd Division, which would be composed solely of black soldiers assembled from among several black National Guard units. But that idea didn't get off the ground until years later, and the 15th remained an independent outfit, along with the Eighth Illinois, and the so-called "separate companies" from the District of Columbia, Maryland, Massachusetts, Connecticut, and Ohio.

The 15th was the pride and joy of Colonel William Hayward, a white lawyer who quit his job as Public Service Commissioner of New York State to get the regiment up and running. He had seen service as a captain in the Spanish-American War, and had since been promoted to colonel in the National Guard in his native Nebraska. He moved to New York to become a partner in a prestigious law firm, and soon afterward became assistant to District Attorney Charles Whitman. When Whitman was elected governor, Hayward went along with him to Albany where he served as his counsel. It was his closeness to the governor that led to the approval for him to form the 15th New York Infantry.

The idea of a colored National Guard regiment had originally been suggested by a local man, Charles Fillmore, whom Hayward promoted to captain after the dream was finally realized. By the time it became a reality on paper, a survey showed that 200 Harlem men were veterans of the Army or of militias in other states. Using them as starting point, recruiting began on June 29, 1916. Ten companies of 65 men each had been formed by October, and that was enough to get recognition from New York State, and for the regiment to be presented with its colors. By the following April, it had reached the required peacetime strength of 1,378, which earned it recognition on the federal level.

The next step was to recruit enough men to get the regiment up to war strength, which required 600 more men. Five days later they were ready to start drilling, including the time it took for them to pass a tough physical examination, which had been set to a higher standard than the rest of the military services. Growth meant that the regiment wasn't exclusively made up of Harlemites any longer. The unit was divided into three battalions of four companies each: the first composed of men from Manhattan, the second of recruits from Brooklyn, and the third divided between men from Manhattan and from The Bronx. "There is no better soldier material in the world," Hayward noted with pride.

He knew what he was talking about. During his service in Cuba during the Spanish-American War, Hayward had commanded black troops whose bravery had left a lasting impression on him. He convinced Governor Whitman to approve a black regiment by drawing on his own battle experiences, but the event that pushed the idea over the top was the gallantry of the Negro troops of the Tenth Cavalry against Pancho Villa's Mexican revolutionaries at Carrizal, in 1916.

Colonel Hayward never left the regiment, but after his men came home from the war, he was appointed United States Attorney for the Southern District of New York, a job he held during most of the Prohibition years before retiring in 1935. But retirement didn't slow him down. The colonel became a big-game hunter. Some of his trophies from Africa are still at the American Museum of Natural History, but he also brought back some live specimens: polar bears from the Arctic for the Bronx Zoo.

A man with that kind of energy was absolutely perfect for giving birth to the regiment in Harlem. But even he wasn't able to get them proper uniforms or rifles to drill with. That took more than three years of cutting through red tape. In the meantime, his men came as they were and used broomsticks for guns. And before they marched off to war, they didn't have an armory where they could drill. At first they used the basement of the Lafayette Theater on Seventh Avenue and West 132nd Street, but they outgrew it within months. After that, they frequently marched in vacant lots, but more often they just took to the streets of Harlem. During spells of bad weather they took cover in local dance halls, and the regiment's official headquarters was in the back of a beauty parlor on Lenox Avenue for a time. The business of the regiment was also conducted at one point from a local cigar store.

The building that is now the Williams Christian Methodist Episcopal Church on Adam Clayton Powell, Jr. Boulevard at West 132nd Street was the first drill hall used by the 15th Regiment, but it had an impressive history before that. It was known for generations as the most important theater in Harlem, the place to see stars like Bessie Smith and Louis Armstrong, and it was where Ethel Waters made her stage debut. A chestnut tree that grew in front of it was called the "Tree of Hope" by out-of-work black entertainers who gathered under it hoping for work, or at least the company of down-and-out people like themselves. Agents looking for talent started gathering there, too, and the tree became a kind of lucky charm. After it was cut down in 1933, a big piece of its trunk wound up backstage at the Apollo Theater, which opened a year later. It is still a tradition for people headed for the stage on amateur nights to stroke it for luck.

Starting out in a theater basement, and improvising as they went along from there may seem to have been a hardship, but it actually had the advantage of making the regiment a part of the Harlem community. They were right out there where everybody could see them and admire what they were going through. It was good for recruitment, too. When the black National Guard units were called into the regular army in the summer of 1917, the 15th New York had 54 officers and 2,053 men. The next largest among them was the Eighth Illinois, which had already seen action on the Mexican border, with 42 officers and 1,405 men. It was all downhill from there. The Massachusetts First Separate Company consisted of 150 men and three officers, and the one from Connecticut had but one officer and 136 men. All of them were eventually brought up to full strength, but alone among them, the men from Harlem were ready to land in Europe at a run when the call came.

The first of these black units to be called into service went on duty six months ahead of the others—before the United States actually declared war, in fact—and the first National Guard unit from anywhere in the country to be called into the regular army in anticipation of the war, The First Separate Battalion of the District of Columbia, was given the job of guarding the nation's capital.

There were dozens of white military units already stationed in the Washington area, and this all-black battalion wasn't even up to full strength at the time. The *Baltimore Sun* gave the reason why it had been chosen in a single sentence: "The Afro-American is the only hyphenate, we believe, who has not been suspected of divided allegiance."

It was considered a great honor to be singled out for a job that down through the history of European wars had always been given to the best and most loyal troops that could be mustered to serve as the palace guard. In this instance, the loyalty of these soldiers was as plain as the noses on their faces. They had been selected *because* of their color, not in spite of it. As the Baltimore *Afro-American* explained it:

. . . There is a whisper going the rounds in the capital of the nation to the effect that the white regiments of the National Guard have so many foreigners, and especially Germans, belonging that the Government was afraid to entrust them with the task of watching over Government buildings of such immense importance as the Capitol, the White House and the houses where the various departments transact their business. . . . A white trooper on guard at some strategic point might be a German-American and be persuaded to let pass a German confederate armed with dynamite to blow up the Capitol. On the other hand, the colored troopers are known as *loyal Americans*, and the army officials are certain that no one can pass their lines, not even the Commanding General, unless he has the password.

Ironically, America's anti-immigrant sentiments had actually worked in the favor of these blacks, giving them a long-denied elevation in status.

After war was declared, the army was willing, even eager, to accept black soldiers at first. But so many black men volunteered that the designated black regiments were brought up to full strength in a matter of weeks. Then the War Department issued an announcement: "No more Negroes will be accepted for enlistment in the United States Army at present. The Colored organizations are filled." The policy would soon change, but part of the problem was that there were almost no black officers in this man's army. There were no plans to change that, and black Americans realized, not for the first time, that if they wanted to fight for their country, they were going to have to fight for the right.

For the most part, the officers who commanded even the all-black units were white. It had been army policy since the Revolutionary War. A notable—and rare—exception in 1917 was the Eighth Illinois, which was sent back to Houston a month or two after the riot there. All of its officers, from corporal on up to colonel, were black men, and nobody was quite sure what was going to happen next.

Its commanding officer, Colonel Franklin Dennison, made it a point to go into town nearly every day to talk with leaders of both races, quietly looking for what he called a "square deal" for his men. He got what he asked for. The pattern was repeated at training camps all over the country, and there were no more riots, although there were some incidents, through the duration of the war. Dennison, as it happened, was the only black senior officer who was sent to France during the war, but he was sent home after a few weeks for "medical reasons."

The fact was that all of the top brass were white men, and that may be the reason why, when Congress authorized fourteen new officer training camps, all of them were restricted to white candidates. At an average of 1,250 officer candidates in each of the new camps, the officer corps would be expanded by 17,500, and every single one of them would be white.

The pleas from the black community for training their people as officers fell on deaf ears until some students and faculty members from Howard University joined with others from black universities in other parts of the country. Their pleas changed to demands for the opportunity to serve their country as officers.

Getting the War Department to listen to those demands wasn't easy, but the brass finally agreed to give it a try, on the condition that two hundred black men with college credentials could be recruited as officer candidates. Although some in the War Department may have thought there weren't that many black collegians in the country, the condition was met. In fact, the Central Committee of Negro College Man presented the department with a list of 1,500 names that it had put together in less than ten days. But they still didn't have their promised commitment.

The next round in the war for recognition was the battle for public opinion. One of the most persuasive press releases said:

> According to the best authorities, about 83,000 new Negroes will be drafted for the New Federal Army. The Negroes welcome this opportunity of serving their country, and sharing their full responsibilities in this time of national peril. They feel, however, that Negro troops thus raised should be officered by men of their own race and are making strenuous efforts to secure a training camp in which such officers can be prepared. The War Department has stated that it is impractical to allow Negroes into the fourteen camps for officers that will be opened on May 14, 1917. And it has also stated that no officers are to be commissioned unless they receive training in one of these camps. This means that unless some provision is made whereby colored men may be trained for officers, these 83,000 Negro troops will be officered exclusively by white men; and that Negroes qualified both mentally and physically to serve as officers will be forced to serve under the conscription law as privates. The colored man is willing and ready to carry out the duties imposed on him as an American citizen, and feels that he should be given the same opportunities in the performance of those duties as are given to other American citizens.

The appeal had some impact among officials in Washington and newspaper editorial-writers, and two days before the officer training camps were scheduled to open, the U.S. Army War College, which had the ultimate responsibility of training officers, announced that black candidates would have their own school after all, and that it would open within a month at Fort Des Moines,

Iowa. The school would accept 1,250 men: 1,000 from the various states on a pro rata basis, and the rest from the ranks of the Regular Army. There was only one minor problem: the list that had been put together by the Howard University committee was composed mostly of college students between the ages of eighteen and twenty-five. The government said it would only accept men between twenty-five and forty. The committee came up with a revised list in plenty of time. At the heart of their direct-mail campaign aimed at older qualified men was that "the race is on trial." It told its prospects: "If we fail, our enemies will dub us as cowards for all time, and we can never win our rightful place."

The school opened on schedule in June 1917. The would-be officers were put through a basic training program tougher than any the U.S. Marine Corps has ever devised. It had been planned that their entire training would last for three months, as was the standard for all such schools. But at the last minute, the authorities extended it by an extra four weeks, assuming possibly, that blacks were slow learners, although no reason was given. The result was that many dropped out of the program. Based on their previous experience with the military system, they had regarded the program as an example of tokenism from the start. In the end, 639 of the original 1,250 received their commissions—106 as captains, and the rest as first or second lieutenants. Then the school, officially known as the 17th Regiment Training Camp, was shut down. There would be no more black officers where they came from.

One of the black noncoms who had been sent there as a military trainer charged that the whole idea of the school at Fort Des Moines had been a sham from the start. " . . . None of the prescribed courses of study given at the other camps were given to the colored candidates," he wrote later. He also charged that the candidates culled from the army itself were, by and large, high-school dropouts, but that they were the ones who were rewarded with the highest commissions. He added to his charge that the college students and graduates among them were treated like "pariahs."

Whether that was true or not, the colored special officer training school was widely considered a failure on both sides of the racial divide, and it may well be likely that the deck had been stacked against it all along.

One clue that critics of the War Department built their case around was that just before the school was to be opened, the man who had been set to command it, Lieutenant Colonel Charles Young, was discharged on medical grounds. The West Point graduate who had become the Army's highest-ranking black officer thought that he was being railroaded. "No one in the regiment, either officer or man, believes me to be sick, and no one save the doctors here at the hospital; not even the nurses. Without one ache or pain, here I sit twirling my thumbs when I should this minute be in Des Moines helping to beat those colored officers into shape." To prove that he himself was in shape, he rode his horse all the way from Ohio to Washington to take his case to the top. He was practically laughed out of town. "All he proved," said one of his critics, "was that his horse was in good shape."

The Howard University students had predicted that 83,000 blacks would be called to serve when the draft law went into effect. They were way off the mark. More than 367,700 of them were drafted into the army during World War I.

Most of them began arriving at training camps in November 1917. An alarming majority of them who had been conscripted through draft boards in the South were illiterate. As the Commission on Training Camp Activities put it: " . . . They were a spectacle to behold. Hundreds coming from the cotton and corn fields or the lumber and mining districts—frightened, slow-footed, slack-shouldered, many underfed, apprehensive, knowing little of the purpose for which they were being assembled and possibly caring less."

Turning these men into soldiers was a discouraging challenge, but the military accepted it by putting the recent graduates of Fort Des Moines into the breach. Their main weapon was night school, where the new men were taught the basics of living and sanitation along with their regular military drills. The special training took five months, but in the end, almost all of them could write their own names, and the majority could read and write a whole lot more. They were also smart on the drill field, their billets were the cleanest in most of the camps where they trained, and they showed remarkable pride, not only in their uniforms, but in themselves. All they had ever needed was a chance.

America formally entered World War I on April 6, 1917. On July 15, the men of the 15th Regiment left their families behind and boarded a train at Grand Central Station bound for Poughkeepsie, New York. There, at Camp Whitman, their new post, they were formally mustered-in to the United States Army.

The next step was formal army training, and the regiment was shipped down to Camp Wadsworth at Spartanburg, South Carolina, where they didn't find a warm welcome from the locals, who said that they were almost duty-bound to teach these New Yorkers to "know their place." The local chamber of commerce filed a protest with the governor of New York, claiming: "The most tragic consequences would follow the introduction of the New York Negro with his Northern ideas into the community life of Spartanburg."

Confrontation came right after they arrived when Noble Sissle, the regimental band's singer and drum major, walked into the local hotel to buy a New York newspaper. The manager walked up to him and ordered him to take off his hat. The soldier's hands were full, with change in one and the paper in the other. When he didn't move quickly enough, the manager took a swing at him and knocked the hat off. When Sissle bent down to pick it up, he took another blow to the head, and as he headed for the door, he was kicked from behind. Other members of the band were on the sidewalk outside and started to rush the place to avenge the insult. Fortunately, James Reese Europe, the bandmaster who held the rank of lieutenant, ordered them all to attention, and a riot was nipped in the bud.

But that wasn't the end of it. The next evening, a group of soldiers assembled at the gate and announced they were going to go shoot up the town. Fortunately, Colonel Hayward was on hand and talked them out of it. He knew, though, that the problem wasn't going to go away. A few days later he went up to Washington for a meeting with Secretary of War Newton Baker. The Secretary's Special Assistant for Negro Affairs went back to Spartanburg with him, where he held a meeting with the regiment's noncommissioned officers. In his report on the meeting, the official wrote: " . . . many of the men, with tears streaming down their faces, approached [me] and voiced how bitterly they felt in the face of the insults which had been heaped upon them as they passed through the town, but at the same time, they told of their willingness to listen the counsel which had been addressed to them for the sake of the Negro race, and for all that was at stake for it and the country during the war."

It didn't solve the problem, and it actually exposed a larger one. The War Department was faced with some tough choices. It could keep the regiment where it was, although local resentment and the New Yorkers' reaction to it didn't show any signs of going away. It could transfer the 15th to another training camp, but that would send a signal to the white community that harassment works. Its third option was to send the unit overseas, even though their combat training had barely begun. The last option was selected, and the regiment was shipped back to New York and then to France.

By midsummer, its Machine Gun Company had landed on Ellis Island in New York harbor with the assignment of guarding captured German spies and suspicious enemy aliens. Two of its companies went over to New Jersey to guard the railroads and keep an eye on war factories; another was assigned to guard the New York Central Railroad's bridges and tunnels for the entire length of the Hudson River; and a third was put aboard captured German ships that had been brought back to New York. The Second and Third battalions were charged with developing the facilities at Camp Upton at Yaphank on Long Island, and at Camp Dix in New Jersey.

On October 12, they were all brought back together again and moved back to Harlem under tight secrecy. Using Fifth Avenue buses, the elevated railroad, and their own foot power, the men boarded boats at the 95th Street Pier on the East River and were taken around to Hoboken, New Jersey, where they boarded a ship bound for Europe. After two days at sea, the ship broke down and limped back to port, so the 15th cooled its heels at several Manhattan armories for the rest of the month.

Again with strict secrecy, they went back to Hoboken, scheduled to sail on November 12 aboard the transport *Pocahontas*. A fire broke out right after they were all boarded, and the ship didn't get under way until December 3. The next day it collided with another ship during a blizzard.

The collision left a gaping ten-foot hole above the waterline, but none of the men was in any mood to go back to Hoboken again, and so they volunteered to take care of the repair job. The captain accepted their offer, and the *Pocahontas* poked along on its eastward course. It could have made faster time, but its sailors were laid low with an outbreak of German measles, which didn't affect any of the troops. It was beginning to seem as if the 15th Regiment was operating under an unlucky star. It is likely that no regiment in the history of the United States Army had ever had such a hard time getting to the front.

But in the end, their luck held and they landed at Brest, France, on December 27, "right side up," as Hayward wrote in his diary.

The troops were transferred to St. Nazaire where they were put to work building a railroad yard, repairing roads, and unloading ships. They put up with it for a while, but more and more, they began asking their officers, "When do we get to fight?"

They thought they had their answer when orders came down to report to Colquidan in Brittany. It was a new artillery camp with plenty of opportunities for action. But it was also a prisoner-of-war camp, and guarding the Germans was what was expected of them.

During the three weeks they were there, Colonel Hayward was pleading their case with General John J. Pershing, the commander of the American Expeditionary Force. The General refused to even consider the idea of an all-black regiment in his army, but offered a compromise by attaching it to the French high command under the formal name of 369th Régiment d'Infanterie États-Unis. Its name identified it as United States Infantry, but its orders from that moment on would come from French officers. Their first orders were to report to Givry-en-Argonne, for the formal transfer and intensive training in a foreign army. In just a few weeks, they outdid their instructors in grenade throwing and bayonet work. They also became surprisingly fluent in their instructors' language.

By May, the men were divided as observers among French units at the front, where they learned the fine points of trench warfare. And in two weeks, they were in the fight on their own, holding a sector at Bois-d'Hauze, Champagne, through the middle of July.

The 369th was beginning to make a name for itself. Before they were through, the enemy would know them well as *blutdürstig schwarze Männer*—"bloodthirsty black men." The men of the 369th called the German enemy "Dutchmen."

3

OVER THERE

World War I was often called the "war to end all wars," but we all know that it didn't work out that way. It was also called the "Great War" and, in terms of casualties, the name surely fits. More than 13 million soldiers and civilians died in the conflict, which was fought largely within the borders of France. Yet it is also a forgotten war. Sadly, many Americans today don't seem to know that it ever happened.

It all started with a chain of events stemming from the assassination of Archduke Franz Ferdinand, heir to the throne of the Austro-Hungarian Empire, by Gavrilo Princip, a young Serbian nationalist. When Austria-Hungary declared war on Serbia, Russia came to Serbia's aid, and that was a signal for Germany to declare war on them, and while they were at it, on its ally, France, as well. When the Germans crossed through Belgium to attack France, Great Britain called it a violation of Belgium's neutrality, and it, too, went to war against the Germans. The colonies of all these countries fell in line behind the powers that controlled them, and for the first time in history, the whole world had taken sides in a war, even though almost nobody was quite sure of the cause they were fighting for.

But there was one exception. The United States said that it was neutral. "It is a war with which we have nothing to do," said President Woodrow Wilson, in his well-known academic style.

Meanwhile, the war went on without the Americans for close to three years. By the time the United States got into the fight on April 6, 1917, it had ground down to a stalemate. The crucial Battle of the Somme the previous November had cost the Germans 650,000 casualties, and the combined British and French forces 615,000 men. The Allies made impressive gains at Verdun a month later, but at a cost of another 550,000 French troops. The Germans retreated, although they were still a formidable enemy. They became even more of a threat on the Western Front after the Bolshevik Revolution took Russia out of the war, and German troops that had been fighting there were shifted over to France.

After the Verdun retreat, the French went on the offensive. General Robert Nivelle predicted, "We shall break the German front at will," in less than forty-eight hours. After ten long days, they had taken only about seventy square miles of territory, which cost the lives of 187,000 soldiers.

It was far from the promised breakthrough, and morale reached a breaking point. The French army mutinied, and more than half of its divisions refused to get back into the fight. By the time the first American soldiers arrived, on June 26, 1917, mile after mile of the front lines had been left dangerously undefended.

The arrival of the Yanks was terrific for morale, but their value as a fighting machine was a matter of opinion, most of it not at all positive. The United Press reported that the first arrivals "are not soldiers." The account said that as soon as they disembarked and before they were herded off into their camps, "They had flirted with every bit of femininity, staged impromptu crap games on the sidewalks surrounded by puzzled natives, and investigated every shop and café." They didn't even *look* like soldiers. The UP reporter noted that their uniforms ". . . reeked of newness. Tunics wrinkled over the chest, trousers were ill-fitting and puttees showed a lack of skill in winding."

Some of them took part in a welcoming parade in Paris, and although the people lining the sidewalks were wildly enthusiastic, one of the onlookers shook his head and said, "If this is what we may expect from America, the war is lost."

The American Expeditionary Force, as it was called, didn't have a single trained division when George M. Cohan wrote: " . . . Send the word, send the word over there/ That the Yanks are coming, the Yanks are coming,/ The drums rum-tumming everywhere." The next line of the song begins: "So prepare . . . ," but many of America's new allies believed that it was already too late.

The U.S. Army hadn't fought a major battle since the Spanish-American War nineteen years earlier, and it had almost no trained soldiers or experienced officers. Secretary of War Newton Baker himself had characterized it as "a profoundly peaceful army."

The problem was compounded by the fact that World War I had broken all the traditional rules of conflict, and no one who hadn't experienced it firsthand could possibly have known what to expect. Among other new weapons, the Germans unleashed chlorine gas on the Western Front, killing troops by the thousands as the wind carried it across the battlefields. Later they would add the even more deadly phosgene and mustard gas, and thousands more would die or become incapacitated for life. The French brought flame-throwers into the mix in 1914, and both sides became adept at using machine guns. Ironically, that weapon had been invented by an American, Richard J. Gatling, back in 1862. Strangely, though, in 1917, there weren't any of the guns in America's arsenal.

The French had also developed a breech-loading cannon that made artillery more important than it had been in any previous war. The missiles they lobbed into trenches and machine-gun nests could deliver smoke or gas bombs, high-explosive shells, or shrapnel. Hand grenades packed with shrapnel were another World War I innovation, but the American army didn't train its men in how to use them.

Tanks and aircraft were also introduced in the Great War, but neither turned out to be much of a menace. Old-fashioned weaponry like sabers and bayonets claimed more victims than planes and tanks put together. But, this was not an old-fashioned war.

The biggest surprise to the military experts was barbed wire. The Spanish had used it as a defensive weapon in Cuba during the Spanish-American War, and in World War I it allowed the enemy to hold off whole regiments with just a couple of men and a machine gun. Any troops attempting to charge an enemy position had to cut through the wire first or find a way around it, and either way, they were vulnerable to defensive fire. There were almost no dramatic infantry or cavalry charges in World War I, although they had been standard offensive procedure for centuries. Barbed wire was another American invention that the Americans neglected to consider when they were getting their troops ready for battle.

Finding men to fill the ranks of those troops was simplified by the Selective Service Act, hastily put into effect in May 1917, a month after war was declared, The new law required every man between the ages of twenty-one and thirty-one to register, and eventually 24 million did. Training them was another story. Camps were built in a hurry; in most cases, recruits were sent to them while the paint was still drying on the new barracks buildings. Uniforms were more often than not delivered in the wrong sizes, and there hadn't yet been any contracts negotiated for the weapons the men would need. In the end it was decided to equip the American troops with materiél made by the Allies. The rifles the soldiers carried were American-made, but they were a modification of the British Lee Enfield rifle, introduced in 1895.

But they muddled through, and ready or not, they began shipping out. In the vanguard of the American Expeditionary Force was the First Division, 15,000 strong. Its commander reported, "Over fifty percent of the soldiers in the division are recruits almost without training."

When the Americans entered the war, the Allied commanders had but one request: "Send us men, men, men."

The first man they sent was General John J. Pershing, the commander of the American Expeditionary Force, whose first job before he was accepted at West Point had been as a teacher in a Negro school near his home in Missouri. The troops he commanded during the Indian Wars were largely black—eleven of them in his cavalry division won the Medal of Honor. As he wrote in his memoirs, "My earlier service with colored troops in the Regular Army had left a favorable impression on my mind . . . and the old 10th Colored Cavalry, with which I served in Cuba made an enviable record there." According to a legend that has built up around him, it was these experiences that earned him the nickname "Black Jack" Pershing.

But when the 93rd Provisional Division, which included the 371st Infantry, made up of black conscripts from South Carolina, and three all-black National Guard regiments, the 369th, 370th, and 372nd, arrived in France, only the 371st was attached to the AEF. The three National Guard units were turned over to the French. It was intended to be a temporary assignment, but they stayed under the French flag for the duration of the war.

The main talent required of a general is that he needs to be a good politician, and at the time, Pershing found himself between a rock and a hard place. He had been deluged with messages from black leaders, some charging him with putting black soldiers in the most dangerous situations, and others putting him down for using blacks only as laborers and stevedores. The latter charge was probably closer to the mark. About 200,000 black soldiers were sent to France during the war, and 150,000 of them served on work details. Either way, though, Pershing's hands were tied. The administration he served in Washington was largely made up of Southerners. President Wilson himself was a Virginian and spent most of his early years in Georgia and South Carolina right after the Civil War, and he never bothered to hide his negative opinion of blacks. At the time, they were not being accepted for service in the navy, the marine corps, or the air service, nor for many specialties in the army, such as the field artillery. That was why the 93rd was called a "provisional" division—it had no artillery unit and no hope of ever getting one. Considering the growing importance of the big guns, it was like asking the men of the Division to fight with one arm tied behind their backs.

Although the Americans were ambivalent about their black soldiers, the French knew exactly what they were getting, and they were pleased by the prospect. They had been fielding colored troops in their army for nearly a century, and France's black soldiers had been in the thick of the toughest fighting in Europe since 1914.

Most of these men were Senegalese and Sudanese warriors recruited from the French colonies in Africa. An official assessment of their performance stated:

> They are particularly apt for attack and counter-attack. . . . The black French soldiers are excellent grenadiers, but they are less prepared in the use of the machine gun and the automatic rifle. . . . These troops are not only devoted to their officers, but they are equally devoted to France, whom they serve most loyally. . . . It is because these soldiers are just as brave and just as

devoted as white soldiers that they receive exactly the same treatment, every man being equal before death, which all soldiers face. In the French Army, white and black wounded soldiers are cared-for in the same hospital by the same personnel.

By the time the Americans arrived, two of France's black soldiers had been promoted to the rank of general, and four had been made colonels. They were part of a special corps called "Bataillons d'Afrique," but the rest of the army called them "Les Joyeux," the happy ones.

The Germans, who called them "Frenchmen from Africa," were never glad to see them. But based on their experience with black troops, the French were more than happy to welcome the new "Africans from America" into their ranks.

In some ways, being turned over to the French might have been the best thing that could have happened to the men of the 369th. The American troops had been sent into the war woefully short on supplies. Although spring was just around the corner, when they arrived it was still cold and snowy in France. But they were told not to expect to be supplied with winter uniforms. The word from Washington was that they needed all the uniforms they could get for the troops that were still in the United States. Pershing compared the situation his soldiers were facing in this war to General Washington's army at Valley Forge.

The black troops assigned to the French army had no such problems. Their uniforms were suited to the weather, and they were even issued boots, which many American troops found nearly impossible to get. They also got better chow. Although the American rations were of better quality than any of the troops that were serving in France, the American army was woefully short of mess sergeants who could turn them into anything palatable. The French, on the other hand, took their cooking very seriously, and the men assigned to their units may not have been as well nourished, but their rations were extremely well prepared, and the meals they were served were the envy of other Allied troops.

The American brass was also suspicious of the French practice of fighting from trenches, and although a French division had been assigned to train the newly arrived Americans in how this war was being fought, Pershing sent them packing. "An American army cannot be made by Frenchmen," he huffed. But like it or not, those Frenchmen understood how this particular war was being waged. The first thing that the men of the 369th learned was how to fight from a hole in the ground, and they learned it from men who been there and done it.

The idea of "digging in" on a battlefield is as old as war itself, but foxholes and trenches had always been temporary affairs until the Great War. Then they became a place to live as well as fight. Some soldiers spent months without ever leaving a trench complex and thousands of them died there. There were hundreds of trenches that stretched in a wide arc for more than 470 miles across the French landscape.

The trenches were slits in the ground about six feet deep and wide enough for two men to pass. They were lined with boards over drainage ditches, most of which provided luxury housing for millions of rats. The trenches along the front of a line were reinforced with sandbags and had steps cut into the forward edge for rifle positions. There were also niches widened out at regular intervals to accommodate machine-gun nests or mortar emplacements.

Just to the rear of the forward line were rows of more trenches, the first of them were intended to provide extra fire support, and those farthest back were service areas, wide enough to accommodate the trucks and ambulances that brought supplies in and carried the wounded out. Every trench complex also included aid stations for emergency medical care, as well as a command post and a communications center that served as home base for flocks of carrier pigeons.

The space between the lines and similar rows of enemy trenches was known as "no-man's-land." It was covered with thick concentrations of barbed wire strung on poles, with land mines buried under them. Nearly every day, portions of the wire would be destroyed by artillery, and nearly every night the soldiers had to go out and replace it. Just before a unit went "over the top" for an attack, some of its men first had to face hostile fire to cut their own wire as well as the enemy's.

When the 369th arrived on the scene, they were sent behind the lines in separate groups of 120 each to a training school where they learned how to use French weapons, including hand grenades and machine guns, which were as foreign to them as the language. On that score, they surprised their new comrades in arms by mastering French fairly quickly. Most of the white American soldiers in France never bothered.

In May, after the first round of training was finished, they were sent to the front lines for intensive training in trench warfare and raiding. Over a two-week period, they were sent in small numbers into battle as observers with every company that went over the top. By the middle of the month, they were sent into action at the Bois-d'Hauze, Champagne, where they were responsible for holding a complete sector without any help from the French. A long section of the line had been abandoned by troops that had mutinied a few months earlier. It was a sink-or-swim assignment, and they came through it swimmingly, although they did sustain heavy losses, during their two months under enemy fire.

After a short rest, the 369th was transferred to Minancourt, where they found themselves in the thick of a German offensive sometimes called the "Fourth Battle of Champagne." Although neither side had much they could brag about in this long war, the

Germans had routed the French in some recent battles along the Marne River, and they had advanced forty miles into French territory. But they were cut off from their supply lines, and on July 15, they moved to expand the territory under their control.

General Henri Gouraud, the commanding officer of the French Fourth Army, which included the 369th, addressed his troops: ". . . The bombardment will be terrible. You will withstand it without weakening. The assault will be fierce. . . . In your breasts beat the brave and strong hearts of free men. None shall look to the rear. None shall yield a step. . . . Your General says to you, 'You shall break this assault and it will be a glorious day.'"

Gouraud was the kind of officer who, as one of his officers put it, made his men "proud to serve in his army." At forty-six, he was France's youngest general, but also one of its most experienced. He lost an arm in a battle at Gallipoli, where he commanded the entire French army. He also broke both of his legs in the battle, and he walked with a limp from a wound he had received earlier fighting in Algeria. His limp and his missing arm would have been enough to make him unforgettable, but he also sported a full red beard. His men would follow him anywhere and when he promised them a "glorious day," they were all confident that it would be . . . and that there would be more glorious days afterward.

The French had learned of the coming attack from captured prisoners of war (brought in by the men of the 369th), and they beat the Germans to the punch by firing the first rounds of artillery with an unprecedented 2,500 guns. It had a devastating effect on the enemy troops already massed for the attack, but it didn't stop them. That would be up to the men in the trenches. General Gouraud had cleared the front line of trenches and filled them with gas canisters and mines to slow the attackers down. The men from Harlem were manning the second row. Twenty divisions of German infantry—more than 280,000 men—charged across the no-man's-land, and there were many instances of hand-to-hand fighting, but they still were not able to break through.

As the enemy retreated, the men of the 369th went up and over and followed them back to their own lines, and during the foray, they managed to find enough abandoned German Mauser rifles to equip a whole brigade. These rifles were similar to the Springfields that the Americans had used for years, and the Hellfighters found them far superior to the weapons the French had issued. They used them for a time with pretty good success, but it was against regulations, and they were soon relieved of them.

The standoff of July 15–17 was the turning point of the war, During five attacks along this same territory, the Germans had lost more than 800,000 men. When it was all over, they were right back where they started from. The French began their counterattack the very next day. By August 6, they had driven the enemy back to the Aisne River. It was a glorious victory for the French. The Fourth Army, with its regiment from Harlem, formed the right flank, east of Rheims.

On September 26 the French Fourth Army formed the left side of a pincer attack from the south, with the American First Army on the other side. A similar attack involving French and British forces came in from the west the following day. The Germans managed to keep the pincers from closing, but they withdrew, and quickly asked for an armistice, which was granted, effective November 11. But that was more than a month away, and the fighting continued, even intensified.

The fighting in the operation which began at Maison-en-Champagne gained as much territory as possible before the shooting stopped. This engagement earned the Croix de Guerre for the 369th Regiment, as well as 171 individual citations for the Croix de Guerre and the Legion of Honor for its officers and men—one of eleven times it was cited for bravery in action. It was the heaviest fighting the men from Harlem experienced in the war. They went into action on the first day with 20 officers and 700 men, but by sundown they were reduced to 7 officers and 150 men.

The battle began at 5:25 A.M. as the French army, with the 369th at its heart, started advancing, and the Americans on the other side began their advance five minutes later. The French were slowed by shell craters that were a reminder of how many other times this Meuse-Argonne sector had been involved in the fighting. They were slowed even more by the presence of German troops on the high ground, manning defenses they had been refining for four years, and by sundown on the first day they had advanced only three miles. By October 1, after three days of fierce fighting, they were still only nine miles from their starting point. Meanwhile, the Americans were having better luck. They met up with four surprised German divisions and managed to push them back five miles along the Meuse River and two miles in the thick Argonne forest. Then their luck turned. German resistance increased as they went along, and by October 1, they, too, seemed to have gone about as far as they could. The offensive was called off for four days.

After the short period of rest and regrouping, the armies were on the march again. Their frontal attacks were costly and slow, although steady. By the end of October, the American side had advanced ten miles from their September 26 starting point, and had driven the enemy from the Argonne forest. Gouraud's French Fourth Army had reached the Aisne River, twenty miles from its starting point. In the meantime, the Germans had brought in their dwindling reserve units to stop the advance, and that weakened their defenses against other Allied offensives that were going on at the same time.

On November 1, the Hellfighters joined the French in an attack on Bourgogne Wood. Although the weather was cold and wet and all the troops were worn out, they advanced another five miles that day and six more the next day. On November 3 they captured a rail line, and prevented a German retreat. But it wasn't over yet. With the Harlem Hellfighters at the forefront, the French force attacked strong enemy rearguard defenses, and eventually reached the Meuse River, closer to Germany itself than any other Allied army. It was as much territory as they would have to fight for. The armistice went into effect the next day, November 11, 1918, at 11:00 A.M. Ironically, the men of the 369th had seen the toughest fighting of the war in the days after the two sides had agreed to stop.

The Allied troops stayed along the armistice line for nearly six more days in order to give the Germans a chance to make an orderly retreat. The Allies also wanted to get supplies up to the line to help civilians in the occupied areas and to care for prisoners of war that the Germans were releasing in wholesale numbers. Finally, on December 1, the Allied armies crossed over into Germany. At the head of French troops, as they crossed the Rhine River into Mainz, were the Hellfighters of Harlem. The black American soldiers had clearly earned the honor of being the first to set foot on the enemy's home soil.

Not long after they got into the fight, the German soldiers became terrified of these black fighters, and the German High Command offered a reward of 400 marks to any of their men who could capture one of them alive. They never succeeded. The 369th was under fire in France for a grater number of days—a total of 191—than any other American regiment. During that time, about 200 of them died in battle and 800 more were wounded. But its Third Battalion alone captured more than 400 enemy soldiers, and although there isn't any complete record, the number of enemy soldiers they killed or wounded was easily in the thousands. One of those captured Germans sounded relieved to have been taken out of the fight. "We can't hold up against these men. They smile when they kill, and they won't be taken alive." It is also often noted that, unique among the fighting men in France, they never lost a foot of ground once they had taken it.

Statistics and battle strategies almost never tell the story of men in combat. Among the stories the men of the 369th proudly told includes the one about the day they were fighting in Belleau Wood back in the spring of 1918. They found themselves under a brutal counterattack, and their French officers called for a retreat.

Colonel Hayward countermanded the order. "Turn back?" he shouted. "I should say we won't. We're going through there or we don't come back." Then he tore the eagle insignia from his lapels, grabbed a gun, and led the company into the fire.

General Gouraud tried to wave him off. "Retire! Retire!" he shouted. Hayward shouted back, "My men never retire. They go forward or they die." Forward they went, and most of them lived to tell about it.

Private Elmer McCowin won a Distinguished Service Cross in the fighting, but he didn't think of himself as a fighter at the time. After he got home, he told a *New York World* reporter:

The Captain asked me to carry some dispatches, and the Germans pumped machine gun bullets at me all the way. But I made the trip and back safely. Then I was sent out again. As I started out with the message, the Captain yelled to bring him back a can of coffee. He was joking, but I didn't know it at the time.

Being a foot messenger, I had some time ducking those German bullets. Those bullets seemed very sociable, but I didn't care to meet up with them, so I kept right on traveling in high gear. None of them touched my skin, though some came pretty close.

On the way back, it seemed the whole war was turned on me. One bullet passed through my trousers and it made me hop, step and jump pretty lively. I saw a shell hole six feet deep. Take it from me, I dented it another six feet when I plunged into it hard. In my fist I held the Captain's can of coffee.

When I climbed out of the shell hole, a bullet clipped a hole in the can and the coffee started to spill. But I turned around, stopped a second, looked the Kaiser in the face, and held up the can of coffee with my finger plugging up the hole to show the Germans they were fooled. Just then another bullet hit the can and another finger had to act as stopgap.

It must have been good luck that saved my life because bullets were picking at my clothes and so many hit the can that at the end all of my fingers were hugging it to keep the coffee in. I jumped into shell holes, wriggled along the ground, and got back safely. And what do you think? When I got back into our own trenches, I stumbled and spilled the coffee.

Daring as that might have been, it wasn't an action that could earn a Distinguished Service Cross. It's what happened next that put a medal on Private McCowin's tunic. He had no sooner arrived back when he went out into no-man's-land for a third time to carry back wounded men. He kept at it until he was gassed, and even then he insisted on going back one more time to rescue a wounded man. During the whole time, machine-gun bullets were whizzing over his head.

Sergeant Bill Butler of the 369th earned his Distinguished Service Cross in the Champagne district in August 1918. A squad of Germans had rushed the trenches and after a short skirmish of hand-to-hand fighting, they captured five privates and a lieutenant of the 369th. As they were making their way to a point where they could all climb out, Sergeant Butler, who was farther down the line, saw them coming and hid behind a turn in the trench until they got to within a few yards of him. Then he opened fire with an automatic rifle. He kept firing until ten of the Germans had been killed; then he went out and captured their slightly wounded lieutenant. After that, he rescued the six Hellfighters who had pressed themselves against the wall of the trench to avoid being hit themselves. They took the five remaining Germans prisoner, and the Hellfighters' record of never having one of their men captured remained intact, although none of these men realized at the time that they were part of one more of the impressive records the Hellfighters established for other military units to envy.

During their time in France some of the noncoms from the 369th were transferred out and made officers in the 92nd Division. While many felt that this was an insult to men who had fought so well together, Colonel Hayward's explanation also summed up how he felt about the men who had served under him:

In August, 1918, the American Expeditionary Force adopted the policy of having all white or all colored officers with Negro regiments, and so ours were shifted away [to join other Negro units]. Our colored officers were in the July fighting and did good work, and I felt then, and feel now, that if colored officers are available and capable, they, and not white officers, should command colored troops. I hope, if the Fifteenth is reconstructed, as it should be, colored men will have the active work of officering it, from top to bottom. There is splendid material there. I sent away forty-two sergeants in France who were commissioned officers in other units. I would have sent others, but they declared they'd rather be sergeants in the Fifteenth than lieutenants and captains in other regiments.

In a letter to a friend in New York, Colonel Hayward wrote:

> They are positively the most stoical and mysterious men I've ever known, And now we have expert opinion. The French officers say they are entirely different from their own African troops and the Indian troops of the British, who are excitable under shell fire. Of course, I have explained that my boys are public-school boys, wise in their day and generation, no caste prejudice, and accustomed to the terrible noise of the subway, elevated, and street traffic of New York City (which would drive any desert man or Himalayan mountaineer mad).—Do you wonder that I love them, every one, good, bad, and indifferent?

But none of that was the real secret of the Hellfighters of Harlem. These were brave and patriotic men who were given a job to do and gave their best to do it right. But then, it didn't hurt a bit that they were New Yorkers, a race of men who know by instinct that it never pays to be above the battle.

4

HENRY JOHNSON'S WAR

Waiting . . . watching . . . wondering. Much more than fighting, these are the things that occupy a soldier's life on the battlefield. The night of May 14, 1918 was a typical example.

The men of the 369th had taken charge of patrolling the front line along the west bank of the Aisne River between Paris and the Belgian border. In September it would become the jumping-off point for the Allies' three-month-long Meuse-Argonne offensive, but on this warm spring evening, the battlefield was quiet. In the trenches behind the barbed wire that crisscrossed it, a five-man squad of Hellfighters had been watching through the night for signs of the enemy, but by 2:30 in the morning there had been almost none. The moon had slipped below the horizon by then, and in the eerily quiet darkness, the men could hear their own heartbeats.

This same squad had stood guard all through the previous night without seeing any sign of the enemy, and there didn't seem to be any reason why the corporal of the guard and two of his men couldn't slip into a trench a few yards to the rear to grab some much-needed rest. They left Privates Henry Johnson and Needham

Roberts behind to act as their eyes and ears, although neither of them was exactly fully rested, either.

It was Roberts who first sensed that something out there in the darkness wasn't quite right, and he slithered on his belly over to his buddy's side. Then Johnson heard it, too—an almost inaudible clicking sound that they both knew was probably being made by a wire cutter. They couldn't see a thing beyond their fingertips, but that sound was enough. It told them that the enemy was out there, even if they couldn't be seen, and the two privates shouted, "Corporal of the guard! Corporal of the guard!"

At that point, Johnson fired a flare to light up the battlefield, but before their eyes could adjust to the burst of light, exploding hand grenades put them in the midst of a shower of shrapnel. The blasts knocked Roberts off his feet, and he was thrown back against the wall of the dugout, badly wounded and not able to get back on his feet.

The grenade barrage also pinned down the other three men in the trench behind them, and Henry Johnson was left to face the German patrol on his own.

He was able to lob a few grenades in the general direction of his attackers, but it wasn't enough to slow them down, and as the first of the German attackers reached the rim of the foxhole, Johnson reached for his rifle. It was a French weapon that held only three cartridges, and his first two shots missed their marks in the darkness. By the time he fired the third bullet, the muzzle of his rifle was pressed against the chest of one of the marauders who reeled backward from the impact and fell dead.

Another German was right on his heels, poised at the edge of the hole with his pistol aimed directly at Johnson's face. All he had to defend himself was his empty rifle, but that was good enough for Henry Johnson. Grabbing it by the barrel, he swung it like a baseball bat, and the butt of the weapon came crashing down on the man's head. As he fell backward, the surprised German shouted—unexpectedly, in English—"The black bastard got me!"

Johnson shouted back, "Damn right! And this little black bastard is going to get you again if you try to get up."

By that point, two more Germans had managed to get behind him, and they were taking Needham Roberts prisoner. Although he himself had three bullet wounds by then, Johnson wasn't going to let that happen. He pulled his bolo knife from his belt, leaped toward the Germans and sank the steel blade into the head of one of them. As he was pulling the bloody knife away, the man he had clubbed with his rifle recovered and was rushing toward him, his Luger spitting bullets. Johnson was hit a fourth time and his knees buckled under him. But before his attacker could finish him off, he lashed out with his bolo knife and drove it all the way to the hilt into the man's stomach.

The carnage gave the rest of the Germans some second thoughts, and all of those thoughts were about making a quick retreat. None of them wanted to tangle with Henry Johnson anymore, but as they were rushing back through the hole they had made in the barbed wire, he gave them something more to remember him by with another barrage of hand grenades.

As the last of them vanished into the night, a relief party arrived to find a half-conscious Private Henry Jonson whispering over and over again, "Corporal of the guard, Corporal of the guard . . . "

Not until sunrise the next morning was a patrol sent out to track down the Germans who had taken on this one-man army. What they found out there made Henry Johnson's war much more incredible than anyone had believed.

The trail the retreating attackers left behind was quite well marked with pools of blood and blood-soaked handkerchiefs and bandages.

It was also littered with abandoned weapons and equipment, including dozens of hand grenades and several Luger automatic pistols. The searchers also found seven heavy-duty wire cutters, possibly including the same one that had alerted Johnson and Roberts to the danger that had come to them in the dead of night.

It was the wire cutters that led Headquarters to the conclusion that Henry Johnson had single-handedly faced no less than twenty-eight of the enemy. They knew that it was standard procedure for the German army to issue one set of the cutters for every four men. On the other hand, what if not all of them had been dropped in the panic of retreat? We'll never know. The Germans took all their dead and wounded with them when they disappeared back behind their own lines, so there is no way of knowing how many men had originally attacked.

The action earned the French Croix de Guerre, France's highest honor for battlefield bravery, for both Johnson and Roberts. It was the first time it had been awarded to any American of any color in the history of the award. Henry Johnson's medal was enhanced with a Golden Palm, a symbol of extraordinary valor that is rarely awarded.

The official citation said that Johnson ". . . has given a beautiful example of courage and activity," and called Needham Roberts ". . . a good and brave soldier."

The regiment's commander, Colonel William Hayward was more expansive in a letter he wrote to Edna Johnson, Henry's wife:

> Your husband, Private Henry Johnson, is in my Regiment, 369th United States Infantry, formerly the 15th New York Infantry. He has been at all times a good soldier and a good boy of fine moral and upright character. To these admirable traits he has lately added the most convincing numbers of fine courage and fighting ability. I regret to say that he is in the hospital, seriously, but not dangerously, wounded. The wounds were received

under such circumstances that every one of us in the Regiment would be pleased and proud to trade places with him.

After describing her husband's heroism and the presentation of the medal in the presence of the entire Regiment, Hayward continued:

> . . . Some time ago, the great General Gouraud [the unit's French commander] placed in my hands the sum of one-hundred francs to be sent to the family of the first of my soldiers wounded in the fight with the enemy under heroic circumstances. Inasmuch as both of these boys were wounded simultaneously, and both displayed great heroism, I think it but fair to send each of you one-half of this sum. Accordingly, I am enclosing New York exchange for the equivalent of fifty francs. I am sure that you have made a splendid contribution to the cause of liberty by giving your husband to your country, and it is my hope and prayer to bring him back to you safe and sound, together with as many of his comrades as it is humanly possible by care and caution to conserve and bring back to America. But it must be borne in mind that we cannot all come back, and none of us can come back until the job is done.

Edna Johnson was also later given the news that her husband had been singled out by former President Theodore Roosevelt, who knew a good fighting man when he saw one, and had placed her husband in his personal honor roll as one of the "five bravest men of World War I."

After the war, Henry Johnson, who had been promoted to sergeant by then, told an interviewer, "There isn't so much to tell" about that May night over there.

"There wasn't anything so fine about it. Just fought for my life. A rabbit would have done that," he said. He also revealed that he had volunteered for the job in the first place:

> The Corporal wanted to send out two new drafted men on the sentry post for the midnight-to-four job. I told him it was crazy to send untrained men out there and risk the rest of us. I said I'd tackle the job, though I needed the sleep.
>
> German snipers had been shooting our way that night and I told the Corporal he wanted men on the job who knew their rifles. He said it was imagination, but anyway he took those green men off and left Needham and me on the posts. I went on at midnight. It was moonlight. Roberts was at the next post. At one o'clock, a sniper took a crack at me from a bush fifty yards away. Pretty soon there was more firing, and when Sergeant Roy Thompson came along I told him.
>
> "What's the matter, men," he asked, "you scared?"
>
> "No I ain't scared," I said. "But I was just letting you know there's likely to be some tall scrappin' around this post tonight." He laughed and went on, and I began to get ready. They'd a box of hand grenades there and I took them all out of the box and laid them all in a row where they would be handy. There was about thirty grenades, I guess. I was going to bust that Dutch army in pieces if it bothered me.

After describing the action that followed, Sergeant Johnson ended the interview, "I was still banging them when my crowd came up and saved me and beat the Germans off. That fight lasted about an hour. That's about all. There wasn't much to it."

No, not much.

Although he had volunteered to replace green recruits that night, Henry Johnson was a little green himself. This was his first taste of combat. Only a few months before, he had been a redcap at the New York Central Railroad's station in Albany, and he had been sent to France after just about a week of combat training. According to the regimental records, that training had extended over a three-week period, but, as was the case with most of the Harlem Hellfighters, shifting of stations had drastically cut into the time he had actually spent getting ready to fight. But that was just a minor detail in Henry Johnson's war.

More than 170 individual officers and men of the 369th were awarded the Croix de Guerre and the French Legion of Honor. The regiment itself earned a Croix de Guerre unit citation for an action at Maison-en-Champagne on September 26, 1918. Two days later, the only black soldier to win America's Medal of Honor in the war distinguished himself on another sector of the same battlefield.

Corporal Freddie Stowers was a squad leader in Company C of the 371st Infantry Regiment, which led an attack on a critical hill. The action had barely begun when the Germans began climbing out of their trenches with their hands over their heads. The Americans ceased firing and came out into the open, but when they reached within a hundred yards of the trench line, the Germans jumped back into their holes and opened fire with mortars and machine guns, resulting in more than 50 percent casualties for the Americans. Corporal Stowers took charge, crawling forward in front of his squad. He made it to a German machine gun nest, and after putting it out of action, called on his men to follow him on to the second trench line. But before he reached it, he was hit by a machine-gun bullet that killed him instantly. Inspired by his bravery under fire, his company pressed the attack and ultimately captured the hill in spite of almost overwhelming odds against them.

There was never any question that Freddie Stowers had displayed the kind of heroism above and beyond the call of duty that is behind every Medal of Honor citation, but his posthumous medal wasn't awarded until 1991.

Henry Johnson is still waiting for his.

The idea that he deserves the honor has been suggested many times over the years, but apparently Johnson's record didn't sufficiently impress the top brass in Washington. The most recent formal request was made early in 2000, and it was approved by the Clinton administration and Army Secretary Louis Caldera. But General Henry Shelton, the Chairman of the Joint Chiefs of Staff at the time, refused to endorse it.

The general rule on awarding the Medal of Honor is that a recommendation must be made within two years of the action, and the actual presentation of the medal must take place within three years for the army and air force and five for the navy, marine corps and coast guard. There are actually three different versions of the Medal of Honor: one each for the army, navy, and air force. The requirements, which differ slightly for each version, have been altered several times since the award was first implemented in 1863, but the time limits still stand, except in certain special cases such as racial discrimination. The medal that went to Corporal Stowers seventy-three years late is one of several historical examples of this rare exception being made.

After Henry Johnson's recommendation was put back on the shelf, that seemed to be the end of it. Once a decision to deny such a request is made, there is no legal apparatus for appealing it. But there may be a special exception in Henry Johnson's case.

His family had always assumed that he had been buried in a potter's field not far from where he grew up in Albany, and that the cemetery had long since been covered up by the runways of the local airport. His war injuries apparently had cost him his civilian job, and he had died broke. But then, early in 2002, Johnson's son

Herman discovered that his father is actually buried at Arlington National Cemetery,

The fact that he was buried at Arlington was a sign to some that the American military had recognized his contribution, and New York's governor George Pataki and its senators Charles Schumer and Hillary Clinton reopened Johnson's Medal of Honor investigation, which under the rules had to be taken back to square one. In the meantime, the Defense Department agreed to posthumously award him the Silver Star, fifth down from the top of the Army's "Pyramid of Honor," ranking below the Distinguished Service Cross and Distinguished Service Medal. The Silver Star is usually awarded for battlefield gallantry just short of the Medal of Honor itself. The award was originally established in November 1918, six months after Henry Johnson earned it.

The wheels grind slowly in Washington, but a White House ceremony in Henry Johnson's honor seems all but inevitable. The official sticking point has been a clause in the law that restricts awarding the Medal of Honor only to heroes of the American armed services serving in their country's wars. Though Americans, the Harlem Hellfighters served in France as a unit of the French army, and that, the officials say, disqualifies Henry Johnson. But there is an exception to every rule. On March 4, 1921, the American medal was awarded to "Unknown" British and French soldiers in ceremonies at Arlington National Cemetery, and they have since been joined by unknowns from Italy, Belgium, and Rumania.

Henry Johnson is far from an "Unknown" soldier. And there is no question that he was a genuine American hero. Whether his government officially recognizes him or not, his name will always be remembered among the people who, as the purpose of World War I was described, helped make the world safe for democracy.

5

C'MON AND HEAR

O n New Year's Day, 1918, when the 15th Regiment first stepped ashore in France, its band struck up a rendition of "*La Marseillaise,*" the French national anthem, but no one in the huge crowd of curious French soldiers and sailors gathered on the pier snapped to attention. In fact, they didn't show any sign at all that they had ever even heard this music before.

The explanation was that they had never heard the music *played* that way before. As the band's leader, Lieutenant James Reese Europe, described it, the realization that this was their national anthem didn't come over them until " . . . after the band had played eight or ten bars."

These Frenchmen had never been exposed to the syncopated rhythms of African-American ragtime, but to paraphrase Al Jolson, they hadn't heard nothin' yet. In the months ahead, they were going to hear a lot more from this band and its unusual style, and they never quite seemed to get enough of it.

By the time James Reese Europe headed home from France, he had become almost as famous on the Continent as General Pershing himself. But when he first arrived there, he was as unfamiliar to the average French citizen as his musical style was. Back home in New York, though, the man everybody called "Big Jim" was a giant among black musicians, and also among white audiences, who considered him to be the successor to Scott Joplin, who had first popularized ragtime music back in the 1890s.

Jim's musical career began in the third grade at a Washington, D.C. public school when he was taught to play the violin. He considered it to be his primary instrument for the rest of his life, but the violin is hardly an instrument that lends itself to marching bands. Yet no boy with even a passing interest in music who was growing up at the end of the nineteenth century could have escaped being caught up in the sounds of martial music. There were more than 10,000 brass bands playing regularly across the country at the time, and Jim Europe's dream of becoming a professional musician was influenced by the greatest of them all.

When Jim was eleven years old, no less a bandleader and composer than John Philip Sousa moved into his family's Washington, D.C. neighborhood. The March King was beginning the process of building the Marine Band into the most respected orchestra of its kind anywhere in the world, but at the same time Sousa was also very interested in developing the musical talents of promising youngsters. At the time, any young person who was seriously interested in becoming a professional musician had to include study abroad to make the dream come true. Sousa realized that such a thing was beyond the reach of many, especially young African-Americans who were beginning to loom large on the musical scene, but were nearly all self-taught. Although the composer of "The Stars and Stripes Forever" was never one to miss an opporunity for self-promotion, he kept his musical training program out of the public eye until the late 1920s, when kids across the country seemed to have suddenly fallen in love with the harmonica. Sousa authorized a version of the instrument to be called the "Marine Band," and he personally wrote ads for it that said: "This instrument is a foundation for a musical career, and many boys and girls who are now learning music on the harmonica will step into the great symphony orchestras and bands of our country some day."

Back when the band's educational programs were just getting started, young Jim Europe was singled out to continue his violin studies under its assistant director. It also gave him an opportunity to study Sousa's style closely, an experience he would eventually put to good use.

When all was said and done, though, Jim still considered himself to be a violinist and he didn't think that there was any future for him in military bands. But he was very interested in black musical theater, and that meant he would have to go to New York if he was going to be able to pursue a career on the stage. Despite reports that there were plenty of jobs there, he quickly found out that unions and booking offices, the traditional ways of finding work, had closed their doors to black musicians, no matter how talented they might be.

Instead, a hopeful like Jim had to go underground. Black performers in those days found jobs by hanging out in clubs, saloons, brothels, and other such places that offered entertainment in the Manhattan neighborhood known as the Tenderloin, along Sixth Avenue, roughly between 23rd and 34th Streets. Many of these establishments invited visiting musicians to perform with their house bands, and enterprising agents, club owners, and others who were in a position to offer contracts, made the rounds of them looking for new talent. But although most of them seemed to like Jim and said that they admired his talent, none of them was interested in hiring him. There was simply no market for fiddle-players in New York. Jim got around the problem by switching to the mandolin and that, along with his talent for the piano, finally landed him enough jobs to at least pay the rent.

Then he hit pay dirt at the Marshall Hotel up on 53rd Street in the neighborhood known back then as "Black Bohemia." It was the unofficial headquarters of successful black entertainers, and although Jim Europe was still an outsider, he caught the eye of John Love, who worked for the prominent Wanamaker family, the owners of huge department stores in New York and Philadelphia. Love hired him and his string quartet, which had been performing at the Marshall, to play for a Wanamaker party, and the family never had another one without Jim Europe's music. More important than good-paying jobs, the association earned Jim a solid reputation among people who mattered in society, in both New York and Philadelphia.

As far as Jim was concerned, though, playing for society parties was just a sideline. He had gone to New York to get involved in the black musical theater, and he got his first break as the orchestra director of the show *A Trip to Africa*. At the same time, with half a dozen published compositions, he was also becoming well known as a songwriter.

Jim Europe was introduced to the intricacies of ragtime through another Marshall Hotel regular, Ernest Hogan, who hired him to play in what he called the "Memphis Students' Orchestra," which performed for two seasons at the Paradise Garden on the roof of Oscar Hammerstein's Victoria Theater in Times Square. None of the players were students, except possibly of ragtime music, and none of them were from Memphis, either. But it sounded good in their ads. So did the music they played. In his book, *Black Manhattan*, written in 1930, James Weldon Johnson noted that the Memphis Students was "the first modern jazz band ever heard on a New York stage." But that was twenty-five years before Johnson's book was written, and the word "jazz" hadn't been coined yet. (Jim Europe himself said that he was the one who invented the word, but he never proved it.) Besides, the "Students'" band was made up entirely of such string instruments as banjos and mandolins. There weren't any of the drums or brass, saxophones or clarinets that usually make up a modern jazz combo.

Jim Europe became one of the most important figures in black musical theater over the next five or six years until about 1910, but when the public's enthusiasm for that form of entertainment began to cool, he and others like him found themselves out of work again. That was when he discovered another one of his talents and became an entrepreneur.

The largely white theatergoing public's mood had turned away from black theatrical enterprises, but its attention was shifting in a big way in the direction of ragtime dances like the turkey trot and the grizzly bear. Suddenly there was a new demand for people who could play the music that could make the dancers move. Jim Europe gave them what they wanted. Along with a few of his Marshall Hotel cronies, he formed the Clef Club and was elected its first president. Harlem newspaper *The Age* gave it a grand sendoff when it reported that it had been formed by "well-known musicians and singers of Greater New York, the majority of whom play and sing in the leading hotels and cafés of New York City, and provide entertainment for the smart set."

The real purpose of the club was to upgrade the status of black musicians and to give them a chance to command higher salaries and better jobs. Its members held fund-raising concerts to finance their new clubhouse, which was on 53rd Street across from their old home base at the Marshall Hotel. Once it was up and running, they started allowing people who weren't in the music business to join the club.

As the Clef Club flourished during the first decade of the twentieth century, it was taking in more than $100,000 a year, mostly from the huge fees that these new members were paying. But those who were wealthy enough to afford it were privileged to be entertained by the city's best black musicians during regularly scheduled members-only white-tie affairs. Of course, the Clef was much more than just a venue for music and dancing. Jim encouraged his musician friends to hang out there, and the club quickly became New York society's major source of musical talent. Before long they were playing for important parties at every first-class hotel in New York, as well as in Paris and London and, of course, Philadelphia, where Jim's solid Wanamaker connection was still paying off big time for him.

Jim's fondest dream at the time was to form an all-black symphony orchestra, and it was one of his new connections that gave him a boost toward realizing it. David Mannes, who was the concertmaster of the orchestra that later became the New York Philharmonic, approached him with the idea of establishing what he called the Music School Settlement, a place where Harlem youngsters could get free music lessons from Clef Club members who would become its faculty. Never at a loss for ideas of his own, Europe suggested that the club's symphony orchestra could raise funds to help establish the school by giving a concert at Carnegie Hall. The orchestra he had already begun to form still needed a lot of fine-tuning, but when Mannes booked the concert hall, Jim went to work with a passion.

Their first concert took place on May 2, 1912, and Carnegie's rafters may still be vibrating from it. The Clef Club Orchestra, which filled every inch of the stage, wasn't anything at all like others that had played there before, or probably since. It had forty-seven mandolins and eleven banjos, plus many of the traditional instruments like saxophones and trombones. It also had fourteen upright pianos, and just to make sure everybody stayed awake, Jim brought in two church choirs to belt out rousing spirituals. The critics were hugely impressed by the concert, but even more so by Europe's scholarly press release that explained what was going on up there on that very crowded stage.

" . . . Other peculiarities are our use of two clarinets instead of an oboe," it said. "As a substitute for the French horn, we use two baritone horns, and in place of the bassoon we employ a trombone." What he neglected to tell the newspapermen was that none of the musicians who made the Clef Club their second home had any idea how to play an oboe, a bassoon, or a French horn. More surprising, considering his affection for the instrument, the orchesta came up shy on violins. There were only eight of those in the Clef Club Orchestra.

It didn't matter. These men were masters of the instruments they were able to play, and the success of the Carnegie Hall concert clinched Jim Europe's reputation. He became not only the most sought-after society orchestra leader in town, but his new fame also gave him a complete monopoly on providing black musical talent for private parties and shows. As Tom Fletcher noted in his book, *100 Years of the Negro in Show Business*, "The colored musicians, all members of the Clef Club, had every amusement place outside the legitimate theaters sewn up."

Big Jim Europe obviously enjoyed his success as a society orchestra leader, but he had always been a man on the lookout for new ideas. When a new opportunity presented itself in 1913, he jumped at it.

The dance team of Vernon and Irene Castle had recently emerged at the top of a new craze for ballroom dancing, and although they themselves were white—Vernon was from England, and Irene from Westchester, a New York suburb—they had become most famous for what Irene called "rough and tumble numbers to ragtime." They appeared at hotel tea dances, at nightclubs, and at private parties. But everywhere they went, they had to settle for whatever orchestra the management or their host provided. They never had any problem with tangos, waltzes, or two-steps, but when the Castles called for ragtime rhythm, the bands generally fell silent. The team danced exclusively for white audiences, and the musicians behind them were often white, too, without a clue what was becoming of popular music behind their backs.

Then one night, the music at a private party was being provided by James Reese Europe's Society Orchestra. The Castles were amazed at what they were hearing. They offered Jim a new permanent job on the spot, making him their personal bandleader. All of their contracts written after that night called for music to be provided by Europe's orchestra.

Their first joint venture was a dance school called Castle House on East 46th Street, where wealthy women paid two dollars for afternoons of dance demonstrations and all the tea they could drink. The lucky ones sometimes got to dance with Vernon Castle himself, but all of them were entertained by the music of James Reese Europe, whom the ladies adored almost as much as they all loved Vernon.

On the heels of that success, the partners opened a supper club called the Sans Souci in Times Square. With a hundred-dollar minimum, it was a little pricier than Castle House, but that didn't discourage the likes of the Vanderbilts and the Goulds, the Astors, Harrimans, and Rhinelanders, and the place was filled to capacity every night. The club was shut down by fire inspectors six months after it opened because it didn't have enough fire exits, but in the meantime, the Castles didn't mind admitting that it had been "a gold mine."

At about the same time that he was making a name for himself at the Castles' clubs, Jim made history again when his orchestra became the first black musical group to sign a contract with a major recording company. One of the first numbers they recorded was the

Castles' signature piece, "Castle Rock," which Jim had written along with his collaborator Ford Dabney. Jim's heart belonged to Vernon and Irene, and the feeling was mutual.

In recalling those days, Irene Castle wrote that Jim Europe was "a skilled musician, and the first to take jazz out of the saloons and make it respectable." She added that, "all the men in his orchestra could read music, a rarity in those days." It was true that the hundred or so Clef Club musicians who worked with the Castles could read music, but that was far from the case among the club's membership as a whole. Most of them played by ear, although their audiences didn't realize it, or didn't care, either.

Back when he was putting together the orchestra for the Carnegie Hall debut concert, Europe confessed to David Mannes that he placed his players in groups around a single music stand, putting one or two who could read music within each group. The others, he said, "simply catch by ear what their neighbors are playing and then join in." But whether they could read music or not, Europe was proud of his experienced men. "They can catch anything if they hear it once or twice, and if it's too hard for them the way it is written, why they just make up something else that will go with it." In a tribute to the rest of the Clef Club orchestras, Jim's friend Eubie Blake wrote: " . . . The Europe gang were absolute reading sharks. They could read a moving snake, and if a fly lit on that paper, he got played."

By 1914, the Castle-Europe partnership was the toast of the New York entertainment scene, and word was beginning to spread across the country that this was a "must-see" attraction. As a way of satisfying the demand, they embarked on what they called the "Whirlwind Tour" of thirty cities in twenty-eight days. Although it was a scaled-down version of their New York show, it took a special train of three pullman cars to move them and all of the band's instruments from one city to another.

The troupe performed twice a day in each of the cities they visited, and the highlight of every performance was a dance contest with members of the audience competing for a trip to New York and a chance to show their stuff at a national championship competition that would be held in Madison Square Garden. The Garden was filled to capacity when the final event took place, but in the end, after a very long, exhausting night of dancing, the winner turned out be a New York couple, who turned out to be the brother and sister-in-law of Wall Street financier Bernard Baruch. That didn't hurt Jim's society image a bit, and the tour that preceded it had spread his fame among middle-class audiences as far west as Omaha.

The most significant accomplishment of the Whirlwind Tour was the introduction of the fox-trot, for which the world had Jim Europe to thank as well. He was intrigued by the slower-tempoed "Memphis Blues," which he had been first to play publicly after it was written by W. C. Handy, and he approached Vernon with the idea that it might serve as an interesting counterpoint to the faster dance numbers like the Castle Walk, that dominated their programs. Jim even described a simple step known as the "get over sal," that he had learned when he was a kid, and which seemed to him to be a perfect match for the music's tempo. Renamed the fox-trot, the step became an overnight sensation. It gave everyone a chance to get out on the dance floor, whether they had much dancing ability or not, and it established the rhythms of most of the popular songs that followed for generations. The fox-trot was the most popular dance step in America for the next fifty years.

Pushing their now-legendary popularity another step forward, Irene Castle put the icing on the cake a week or two after the tour when she had her hair bobbed, and thousands of women across the country rushed off to the hairdressers for new hairdos. The hairstyle, which hadn't been seen very much before Irene got her hair cut, remained popular for years to come and it became one of the symbols of liberation for the young flappers of the 1920s.

Having conquered the United States, the Castles began planning a European tour scheduled to culminate with the opening of a supper club in Paris that they intended to make into a home away from home for Jim's orchestra. But the plan had to be scrapped when the Great War arrived on the Continent first.

James Reese Europe was a human dynamo, and when that foreign tour was canceled, he didn't lack for things to do. He was still providing music for the Castles, a full-time job in itself, but he had a lot of other irons in the fire as well. The instrumentation of his symphony orchestra had evolved into something more traditional by then, and he was hard at work putting together concerts of serious music by black composers. He was also deeply interested in making the Music School Settlement the pride of Harlem. At the same time he had become the musical director of the Broadway show called *Watch Your Step*, and he wrote some of the music for another called *Darkydom*, which, although a flop, led to his association with Noble Sissle and Eubie Blake, whom he met when they took the show on the road. All the while, of course, Jim and his men were still involved in a big way in an endless round of society parties.

Then, in the midst of it all, Jim Europe enlisted in the new 15th Regiment as a private. He was obviously much too busy to take the time for drilling and training in the machine-gun company that he was assigned to, but he still took on the assignment with his typical enthusiasm. The reason he gave for joining in the first place was that, "Our race will never amount to anything, politically or economically in

New York or anywhere else, unless there are strong organizations of men who stand for something in the community."

Although Jim had joined up as a statement of support for the outfit, his commanding officer, Colonel William Hayward, had bigger plans for the musician than teaching him to handle a machine gun. He needed a man who could help with his recruiting efforts, and he believed the Almighty had just dropped one into his lap. There was plenty of community support for the regiment, but Hayward needed more men to fill its ranks, and he knew that the best way to get them was to dazzle them with a big brass band.

Meanwhile, Jim had passed the examination to be commissioned as a lieutenant, and the army didn't allow officers to be bandleaders. But Hayward didn't want Europe to lead his regimental band, just to put one together. Jim wasn't at all interested in the proposition, though, and he turned it down flat. Then he reconsidered, but on terms that he may have believed would scotch the idea anyway.

First of all, he said that the 15th's band had to be the best of any in the army because his reputation would suffer if he were to be associated with any second-rate outfit. That obviously meant hiring professional musicians, but Jim softened the blow by pointing out that he would only need a few key men to set the standard for the others. This handful of professionals wouldn't actually be members of the regiment but would be like the trained singers that are often hired for church choirs. That meant they would have to be paid outside the regimental budget, and Jim told Hayward to expect an extra expense in the neighborhood of $15,000 to get the band up to speed.

Europe's second demand was that this band was going to have to have at least fifty-four players, if not sixty, even though army regulations limited the size of regimental bands to twenty-eight. That meant that Hayward was going to have to bend the rules, but he didn't waste any time coming up with a solution.

He decided to bump up the roster by making playing in the band a "special duty." As long as the musicians were available for their regular assignments, it wouldn't matter to the army how big the band got to be. That also meant that Jim Europe could be the band's leader in spite of his commission. As far as the regiment's table of organization was concerned, Jim was listed as the commander of a machine-gun company.

That wasn't the end of the problem, though. The army wouldn't supply instruments and scores for a band with more than twenty-eight members, so that would cost even more money. Fortunately, Colonel Hayward had a rich friend. He asked Daniel G. Reid, a board member of U.S. Steel, to write him a letter of introduction to twenty of his friends who might be willing to contribute to the cause. Instead, Reid wrote him a check for $10,000 and said, "Here are your twenty victims at $500 apiece." The band was on its way.

Europe's first recruit was his close friend Noble Sissle, the songwriter and singer, who became the 15th's drum major. Bert Williams, who was starring in the Ziegfeld Follies at the time, was already a member of the regiment, and he, too, was among the first to be signed up for special band duty. Williams had begun his career in vaudeville as a member of Gus Edwards' School Days, a troupe made up of schoolboy partners George Jessel, Eddie Cantor, and Walter Winchell. In the 1920s he was one of the top stars of silent movies, and he was still appearing in Broadway shows into the 1950s.

Jim knew every black musician in the city, but as he had discovered when he was building his orchestra, not very many of them were able to play reed instruments like clarinets and saxophones that were key to making the difference between a military band and an ordinary drum-and-bugle corps. But if he couldn't find them in

New York, he knew that there were a lot of them among black musicians in Puerto Rico. He took a trip to San Juan to persuade the musicians to join the New York National Guard. The trip paid off. He went home with thirteen of the best reed players on the island after only three days of searching.

While he was away, Sissle signed up Francis Mikell, who had taught music at the Tuskegee Institute and had wide experience as a theatrical music director. He would be named as the regiment's bandmaster and, as Europe's assistant, he was put in charge of whipping the band into shape.

Less than a month after rehearsals began, the band was considered good enough to give the first public concert in a series that was intended to raise funds to pay the salaries of the professional musicians who weren't on the regiment's official roster. They also frequently marched in New York parades, right up to the one that took the regiment to the pier where they caught their ship bound for France.

After the 15th arrived overseas, it was assigned to work details, which disappointed the men and infuriated Colonel Hayward. But all of his requests for reassignment seemed to be falling on deaf ears at AEF Headquarters, until the day when Hayward discovered that he had a secret weapon in his regimental band.

The American high command had issued an order that every soldier with combat duty should be allowed one week off for every four that he served in battle. Cities like Paris, with their dangers of rowdyism and venereal disease, were placed off-limits, and the YMCA started setting up special camps where the doughboys could be entertained while they stayed out of trouble. The first of them was at Aix-les-Bains, a resort town near the Swiss border.

The camp's management was looking for entertainment that would remind the boys of home, but there was precious little of that to be found in eastern France. The run-of-the mill bands attached to the American army didn't have much to recommend them. Then the camp's officials got to hear Jim Europe's outfit play, and suddenly nothing else would do. This band's ragtime beat was different from all the others, and it had professional singers and dancers, too. It was like a self-contained vaudeville troupe. General Pershing personally signed the order, and the band was transferred to Aix-les-Bains in time for the camp's opening.

The rest of the regiment was left behind at St. Nazaire, but Hayward was quite confident that the musicians were going to make an important impression on the general staff, and that it would incline them to accept his request for reassignment. But he started out with a handicap. Headquarters ruled that Jim Europe was a machine-gun officer and not a bandleader and they ordered him to stand down with the rest of the regiment.

But one of the top generals on Pershing's staff had heard the 15th's band several times under Francis Mikell, the bandmaster Noble Sissle had signed up, and who served as its leader when Jim Europe was off working with his machine-gun company. While Mikell was good, Europe was much better, and Hayward invited the alrready-impressed general to a concert with Jim wielding the baton so that he could impress on him that an opportunity was being missed. The general got the point and, more important, he convinced Pershing that this band without Jim Europe was like a cannon without shells. Jim was on the train when the band left town. By then he had an official order in his pocket that named him the band's permanent director, at least for this tour of duty.

On its way across France, the train made a stopover at Nantes, where the band gave its first concert for French civilians, at the local opera house. After that, word preceded them up the line, and people were crowding the station platforms at every town they passed through demanding to hear this wonderful music from America for themselves. One of the most important of these impromptu concerts was for the American general commanding the area, and one more vote was cast in favor of the 15th at AEF Headquarters. In spite of the unscheduled stopovers, the band arrived at Aix-les-Bains before the first contingent of battle-weary soldiers pulled into the station.

Jim Europe's orders called for a two-week tour of duty at the camp, but after a day or two of concerts, it was extended for another two weeks. The band not only played for their fellow Americans, but they also scheduled appearances in nearby towns where the local citizens showered them with affection, not to mention bottles of champagne and bouquets of flowers. It could easily have been arranged for the band to stay at the camp for the rest of the war, but like their buddies back at St. Nazaire, the musicians were all anxious to actually get into the fight. That was going to happen sooner than any of them expected.

While they were away, thanks to the attention they were getting, Colonel Hayward had finally been successful in getting a combat assignment for the 15th Regiment. The first inkling the band members had of it was that their orders directed them to report to the 16th Division of the French army, not at St. Nazaire, but at Connantre in the Marne Division, right in the middle of the Western Front. It wasn't until they arrived there (after having stopped to give command performances for the citizens of every town along the way) that they discovered that the 15th New York no longer existed, but was now the 369th, and they had become honorary French soldiers themselves. And that they had arrived just in time for combat training.

Like their stateside training, the regiment's overseas indoctrination was cut short.

Less than three weeks after arriving in the sector, Lieutenant James Reese Europe became the first black American officer to go into battle since the war began.

He did double duty that day. The band accompanied the regiment out of the town to the road that led to the trenches. As they always did on such occasions, they played the French and American national anthems, followed by "The Stars and Stripes Forever." Then they broke the mood with a jazzed-up ragtime rendition of "Army Blues." The anticipated German attack never materialized on that first mission, but Jim was back in action again not long afterward. This time it was a walk through no-man's-land.

It all started as a joke, but it ended up as a lesson to Jim Europe that what passed for wit in America wasn't exactly the same thing here in France. He didn't expect to be taken seriously when he laughingly told a French officer, "I sure wish I could be going out there with you when you scout those German trenches," but the next thing he knew, there he was, crawling under barbed wire with artillery shells whizzing over his head. Later he told Noble Sissle, "Goodness gracious, I knew my time had come . . . talk about hugging the ground. Boy, no sod ever hung as close to Mother Earth as I was." The experience led him to write "On Patrol in No Man's Land," which became a standard at most of the band's concerts after that.

While Europe was serving in combat, most of his bandsmen were behind the lines, playing for regimental ceremonies and for a growing number of military funerals, as well as staging concerts for French troops and civilians. But although it was Bandmaster Francis Mikell who was putting them through their paces, it had become famous as "Jim Europe's band." Then it became famous back home, too.

Among the visitors they entertained was a contingent of war correspondents that included Irvin S. Cobb, well known not only as a writer, but as a racist. The band thought that he was going to be tough nut for them to crack, but they needn't have worried. In an article that appeared in the *Saturday Evening Post*, Cobb put his old prejudices aside and wrote:

If I live to be 101, I shall never forget that second night, which was a night of a splendid, flawless full moon. We stood with the regimental staff on the terraced lawn of the chief house in a half-deserted town five miles back from the trenches, and down below us in the main street, the band played plantation airs and hundreds of Negro soldiers joined in and sang the words. Behind the masses of upturned dark faces was a ring of white ones where the remaining natives of the place clustered with their heads wagging in time to the tunes . . . . When they got to "Way Down Upon The Swanee River" I wanted to cry, and when the drum major [Sissle], who had a splendid baritone voice, sang, as an interpolated number, "Joan of Arc," first in English and then in excellent French, the villagers openly cried; and an elderly peasant, heavily whiskered, with tears of joyous and and thankful enthusiasm running down his bearded cheeks, was with difficulty restrained from throwing his arms about the soloist and kissing him.

Later in the same article, Cobb described the band on parade: " . . . when it played the 'Memphis Blues,' the men did not march. The music poured in at their ears and ran down to their heels, and instead of marching they literally danced their way along. I think surely this must be the best regimental band in our army. Certainly it is the best I have heard in Europe during the war."

Considering his prejudices, that was better than high praise, but Irvin Cobb had been denied the pleasure of hearing the band conducted by James Reese Europe. Jim was at the front at the time, and before long he would be in a field hospital, the victim of a German gas attack. Although most soldiers who experienced gas attacks either died on the spot or were incapacitated for life, Jim Europe was one of the lucky ones. Apart from a painful hacking cough, he hadn't been seriously affected by the poison gas, but the damage to his lungs was serious enough to bar him from frontline active duty for what remained of the war.

Instead, he was transferred to Paris for rest and recovery, and while he was there, he was reassigned, along with the regiment's other black officers, to the newly formed all-black divisions of the U.S. Army. It might have been the end of the road for his band, but the order was canceled almost as soon as it had been issued. Nobody knows with any certainty why the high command changed its mind and rewrote the rule to allow commissioned officers to lead regimental bands, but it seems obvious that Colonel Hayward had pulled a few strings, something he was quite good at doing. On the other hand, though, one of the key officers on Pershing's staff was a member of the Wanamaker family that had been Jim Europe's strongest backers since his career began, and it may be likely that Jim himself could have engineered the policy change himself by calling on his Wanamaker connection. Nobody knows exactly why it happened, but Jim remained a part of the 369th.

Europe had no sooner been called back to his old outfit than Hayward ordered him right back to Paris to conduct an important concert. The Allied leaders were holding a conference there, and the band was expected to be on hand to entertain the dignitaries. Recalling their first concert, in an interview with the New York *Tribune*, Jim said that, "Before we had played two numbers the audience went wild. General Bliss [Pershing's representative at the conference] and the other high officers insisted that we should stay in Paris, and there we stayed for eight weeks."

During those weeks the band played in hospitals and camps along with the best musical outfits of all the Allied nations. Their sojourn came to a climax with a concert program at the Tuileries Gardens where they were to make an appearance along with what were considered to be the best military bands on the Continent: the British Grenadiers' Band, the band of the French Garde Républicain, and the Royal Italian Band. In his *Tribune* interview, Europe said, "My band, of course, could not compare to with any of these, yet the crowd, and it was such a crowd as I never saw anywhere in the world, deserted them for us. We played to 50,000 people at least, and, had we wished it, we might be playing yet." He added, "After the concert was over, the leader of the band of the Garde Républicain came over and asked us for the score of one of the jazz compositions we had played. He said he wanted his band to play it."

Try as they might, although it was highly regarded as one of the most accomplished bands on the Continent, the French musicians couldn't manage to duplicate the 369th's sound. They became convinced that it must be because the Americans weren't using standard instruments but, on close inspection, they had to admit that they had been mistaken. The secret, of course, was style, and that couldn't be taught in any of the music conservatories. Hundreds of writers have tried to put it into words, but Jim Europe warned them that it probably couldn't be done, any more than it could be made apparent on a printed musical score. "It is all in the performance," he said.

"With the brass instruments we put in mutes and make a whirling motion with the tongue, at the same time blowing full pressure," he wrote when he was asked to explain the phenomenon. "With wind instruments we pinch the mouthpiece and blow hard. This produces the peculiar sound which you all know. To us it is not discordant, as we play the music as it is written, only that we accent strongly in this manner the notes which would normally be without accent. It is natural for us to do this; it is, indeed, a racial characteristic."

The Paris concerts were the last the French heard of this "peculiar sound" from Jim Europe's band, but Jim and his men had planted jazz firmly on French soil, and it marked the start of a love affair between the French and jazz music that hasn't cooled yet. That was part of Jim's hopes for the future. He believed that their success could eventually lead to the acceptance of his Black National Symphony Orchestra, back home, and he had high hopes that it would also set the stage for a rebirth of the black musical theater, which was still his first love.

As soon as he and the boys in the band were discharged from the army in February 1919, the day after their triumphal march up Fifth Avenue, Jim announced that the 369th Regimental Band wasn't going to be broken up, and that it would tour the United States to treat their fellow Americans to the same experience the French had enjoyed. After that, he said, they were going to go abroad again for a tour starting in London, where the Prince of Wales had already personally requested their presence.

Some of the men from the original Hellfighters band went back to their civilian careers, and Jim beefed up the organization with more singers and dancers as well as new instrumentalists. But it was still essentially the same band that had marched up Fifth Avenue for the regiment's homecoming. On March 16, 1919, a day short of a month later, they appeared in public again for a concert that filled every seat and every foot of standing room at the Manhattan Opera House, a variety theater on 23rd Street near Sixth Avenue. For the families of the members of the regiment, it marked the first time they had been allowed to sit in the orchestra section of a theater rather than being relegated to the high balconies in the rear, known vulgarly as "nigger heaven." After repeating the program at the Brooklyn Academy the following night, the band's ten-week tour of eighteen cities began the following week, with an appearance at Philadelphia's Academy of Music. That was followed up with the first band concert ever staged at the venerable old Boston Opera House.

Everywhere they went, the local music critics were bowled over. They couldn't seem to make up their minds what they loved best:

the sound of the music or the appearance of the band's six-foot-tall leader who appeared in full uniform, and who was described by one of them as the "peppiest and and snappiest" bandleader the United States had ever produced.

They settled in for a full week of sold-out concerts at the Auditorium Theater in Chicago, where the critic from the city's most important black newspaper, *The Defender,* gushed that after having seen nearly every big concert in Chicago for more than a dozen years, "The work of the 'Hellfighters' would not suffer by comparison with the best of them. In many ways, it would surpass them all: for it is safe to say that no other organization in the world could compete with this one in the rendition of 'blues,' 'jazz,' and Negro folk numbers."

After Chicago, the band headed back east for return engagements in Boston and Philadelphia, and ending with a grand homecoming finale in Harlem at the Manhattan Casino. During their first afternoon concert in Boston, word came down that Massachusetts Governor Calvin Coolidge had invited the band to play at the State House the following morning in a tribute to the 54th Massachusetts Volunteers, the Union Army's first all-black regiment in the Civil War. Jim was honored at the prospect; but, as it turned out, this was a date that wouldn't be kept.

One of the showstoppers in the Hellfighters' concerts was a duel between two drummers, Herbert and Steve Wright. Although they were brothers, this wasn't any display of brotherly love, but rather a genuine fierce competition. On the night of May 9, 1919, Jim Europe found himself caught in the middle of it.

According to one version of a story that has produced several, after they went off-stage for the intermission, the brothers followed their leader into his dressing room, and started complaining about how they were being treated. Jim managed to calm them down, but Herbert still didn't seem to be satisfied. "I work hard for you," he said, "and you don't treat me right. . . . And yet, Steve make all kinds of mistakes and you don't ever say anything to him." Then he threw his drum at the wall and shouted, "I'll kill anybody that takes advantage of me. Jim Europe, I'll kill you." With that, he pulled a penknife from his pocket. Jim grabbed a chair to defend himself, but he seemed to have second thoughts and then put it down. At that moment, Herbert Wright lunged at him and stabbed Jim in the neck. Then he turned and calmly left the room.

When Noble Sissle arrived on the scene a few minutes later, Jim had wrapped a towel around his neck to try to stop the blood that was gushing from the wound. But Sissle said that he was calm and alert and after ordering the second half of the concert to go on without him, he reminded his friend that they had an important date down at the State House first thing in the morning. But before the night ended, Big Jim Europe was dead.

The band that played for his funeral procession in Harlem was not the one he that had taken on tour, but the New 15th Infantry Regiment Band of the New York National Guard, which included the war heroes Henry Johnson and Needham Roberts. The "Jimmy Europe Jazz Band," led by his longtime partner, Ford Dabney, marched at the end of the procession wearing black armbands and carrying their instruments silently at their sides.

There were dozens of eulogies delivered that day, but the one that the *Tribune* singled out as the most appropriate was made by Jim's old friend, Deacon Tanney Johnson, who said, "Before Jim Europe came to New York, the colored man knew nothing but Negro dances and porter's work. All that has changed. Jim Europe was the living open sesame to the colored porters of this city. He took them from their porter's places and raised them to positions as real musicians. I think the suffering public ought to know that in Jim Europe, the race has lost a leader, a benefactor, and a true friend."

Big Jim Europe was thirty-nine years old when he died. His whole life was still before him, and the future couldn't possibly have looked brighter. Soon, all of his associates went off in other directions. Eubie Blake and Noble Sissle teamed up as a vaudeville act performing their own songs as what they called the "Dixie Duo," and then they went on to follow Jim's dream of reestablishing black musical theater with *Shuffle Along*, which opened the door for more shows like it that were written and performed by black artists.

More acceptance for black entertainers followed, with the emergence of such stars as Paul Robeson, Fletcher Henderson, Bill "Bojangles" Robinson, and Duke Ellington. The new medium of radio helped to spread their popularity, and musicals like Jerome Kern's *Show Boat,* and George Gershwin's *Porgy and Bess,* swept away the color lines from the world of popular entertainment.

Jim Europe would have been proud. That had been his lifelong goal. And he would have been especially pleased with the Jazz Age that emerged not long after he died. It took the whole world by storm, but the world might never have had a chance to enjoy the experience if James Reese Europe hadn't laid its foundation.

6

THE NEW NEGRO

After the doughboys came back from the Great War, the blacks among them who had grown up in the South expected that they were going to find attitudes changed, but it didn't take very long for them to find out that they had been wrong. Many of their former white neighbors appeared ready to welcome them home to the South with open arms, but there was an undercurrent of fear among most Southern whites that these men who had been given a taste of democracy over in France weren't going to hold still for the kind of treatment they had experienced before the war. They themselves didn't see any reason to change their own attitudes. They were also resentful that so many blacks had left for better jobs up north, leaving them with an economy-wrecking labor shortage.

Most of the black working class had gone to industrial centers like Detroit or Chicago after the beginning of the twentieth century, but New York was starting to become a destination for them, too. The city had never been a mecca for Southern blacks, at any time in its history, although the roots of its own African-American population dates back to 1628, less than ten years after the first black slaves were brought to the Colonies, down the coast at Jamestown, Virginia.

Nearly all of the blacks in the Dutch colony of New Amsterdam had been captured in pirate raids on Spanish and Portuguese ships, and all of them were involved in public-works projects like building roads and forts. The Dutch West India Company, which controlled everything, found it more profitable to sell their human cargo down in the Caribbean. Yet, by the time the British took over in 1664, about 10 percent of the eight thousand new New Yorkers were blacks, and many of them had already earned their freedom. The English saw the profit potential in the slave trade and encouraged the importation of Africans. By the eve of the Revolutionary War, almost seven thousand of them had come to America through the port of New York, and slave markets at the foot of Wall Street were busier than any in the Southern colonies, with the single exception of Charleston, South Carolina. By the time slavery was outlawed in New York in 1799, the city's black population was well over three thousand, a little more than 14 percent of the total (compared to about 25 percent today).

Just before the dawn of the twentieth century, the descendants of these families were joined by migrants from the South, mostly from Virginia or the Carolinas. But with the coming of World War I, and in the years that followed, they were arriving from as far away as Mississippi and Alabama, looking for freedom and a better way of life in the home of the Hellfighters.

A new age seemed to have dawned that cold morning in February 1919 when the Hellfighters marched up Fifth Avenue. Journalists, politicians, and ordinary Americans never seemed to run out of good things to say about them, as well as African-Americans in general. It seemed as though racism was finally on the run at last. At the very least, the Hellfighters had lit the spark of black pride in the City of New York.

A few months later, during the summer of 1919, Americans found a new menace in the form of communists, anarchists, socialists, and anybody in their neighborhood who had a foreign-sounding name. U.S. Attorney General A. Mitchell Palmer formed a new branch of the Justice Department and began to round up suspected radicals, jailing those who were citizens, and deporting those who were not. Blacks, who had become all too familiar with repression and denied justice like this, paid almost no attention to this so-called Red Scare, but the national mood of hate and suspicion it created had a corollary in a new rebirth of racism.

It reared its head in Charleston, South Carolina, only about a dozen weeks after the 369th arrived home to New York, when the U.S. Marines had to be called out to put down a race riot. Not long afterward, three thousand Mississippians showed up to cheer on the lynchers of a young black man who had been accused of rape, even though he had never been tried for the crime. That event, however, wasn't a spontaneous example of mob rule, but had been carefully planned and then reported in advance by the local newspapers. It was only one of seventy-seven lynchings that took place during that summer. Of those, ten were veterans of the war. A few of them were hanged still wearing their uniforms.

This reign of terror touched more than twenty-five American communities that summer, including Washington, D.C., where the riots went on for two days. In Chicago, thirty-eight people were killed on both sides during a five-day race war; 537 were injured, and more than a thousand blacks looked on as their homes were burned to the ground. It was as though the World War had never happened, as if no black men had given their lives to put an end to such things, even though 404,308 African-Americans served in the U.S. Army during the war, and 42,000 of them saw combat in spite of the fact that it was the army's policy to keep them away from the front lines. Many of those men came back wounded, and many didn't come back at all. The 369th Regiment alone suffered 35 percent casualties.

What the war had changed, though, was the response to incidents like those among black leaders. Former slaves and their children had been enduring them since Emancipation with patience and fortitude, and most of them had become resigned to the fact that it was futile to fight back. But the combination of the excesses of the Red Scare and the realization that racist attitudes were just as nasty as they had ever been, proved to them that if they chose to fight, they were going to be taking on a formidable enemy. At the same time, though, they came to the realization that it was the whites who had the problem, and nothing was ever going to change unless they themselves worked to bring about an attitude adjustment. But that meant that they would have to take their lives into their own hands.

The militant *Challenge* magazine, sounded one of the first calls to battle in an editorial that proclaimed: "The German Hun is beaten, but the world is made no safer for Democracy. Humanity has been defended, but lifted no higher. Democracy will never be safe in America until these occurrences are made impossible, whether by the proper execution of the law or with double-barrel shotguns."

Nearly every other black newspaper and magazine across the country echoed the sentiment. All of them proclaimed the birth of the "New Negro," whose changed attitude, they predicted, was going to alter the course of American history. But at the same time, most of them cautioned that double-barreled shotguns could backfire if they weren't handled with care.

As far back as 1903, W. E. B. Du Bois started advancing the idea that the Negro's salvation was going to come from an educated group of the brightest and best of the black race which he called the

"Talented Tenth." Its influence on the masses, he wrote, "could guide the American Negro into a higher civilization."

His idea was echoed and moved forward after the war by Charles Johnson, the editor of the Urban League's magazine, *Opportunity*, who wrote that African-American artists and intellectuals held the key to exposing stereotypes and prejudices to the sunlight. He was convinced that once those old ideas were swept away through positive, creative thinking, blacks as well as whites would start to realize the positive contribution that the Negro race had to offer the country.

Johnson's theory was based on his conviction that blacks were an inherently artistic race, just as Jews seemed to have a natural talent for business, Muslims for science and philosophy, and Anglo-Saxons for building empires. If blacks were being excluded from positions of power in the business world, and denied such basic civil rights as voting, he pointed out, there still weren't any barriers to them in the worlds of music and literature. It represented an open door that needed to be pushed open even wider.

At the time, there may have seemed to be no better proof that Johnson was on the right track than the success of Jim Europe's 369th Regiment Band. The regiment's battle record had earned it the sincere respect and admiration among most Americans, but people generally admired the musicians even more. Their public appearances brought a whole new life to black music, as well as new respectability to the men who played it. They also were responsible for bringing about a rebirth of black theater, and Europe alumni Eubie Blake and Noble Sissle were leading the way with their hit Broadway musical, *Shuffle Along*.

While the excitement was at its peak, *Variety*, the show-business Bible, reported: "The 1920's have brought stature to Harlem. In a remarkably short time, it has been made one of the best-known spots in the entire world. Among the reasons have been the commercial progress of the New York Negro; the international fame of its theatrical celebrities; the stage pieces that include its atmosphere; and books having the section as its locale."

Thanks to men like Jim Europe, black musicians had already been internationally famous for years, but what this new renaissance was bringing into the mix was Harlem's community of writers. One of the first of them was Jamaica-born Claude McKay, who touched a nerve in the community with a defiant sonnet, "If We Must Die," which was written as the 1919 race riots were sweeping the country. "If we must die, let it not be like hogs/ Hunted and penned in an inglorious spot," he wrote, and his words became black America's call to arms. But as other black writers and poets began migrating to Harlem, the neighborhood was starting to turn into something that was the direct opposite of "an inglorious spot."

The movement, whose goal was to prove that blacks were "civilized," was boosted through the works of writers like W. E. B. Du Bois, Charles S. Johnson, Jessie Redmon Fauset, and James Weldon Johnson, all of whom created a strident drumbeat celebrating black creativity in newspapers and magazines. At the same time, Alain Locke, the first African-American Rhodes scholar, already a well-known writer and a professor at Howard University, proposed that graphic artists should study African art and then popularize it in America. He expanded his call to include wealthy patrons who came forward more than willing to subsidize the effort, and in the same vein, novelist Carl Van Vechten began to introduce promising new writers to white editors and to other successful writers of both races. He also organized a literary competition that offered cash prizes along with publishing opportunities that resulted in new books of poetry by both Langston Hughes and Countee Cullen.

Hughes, whose later works of fiction centered around the lives of black characters, wrote "Mulatto," a play that ran on Broadway for two years. He was also a songwriter. During World War II, he toured Army bases with the USO, reading selections from his own writings. Cullen, a graduate of NYU and Harvard University, spent part of his writing career in Paris after having won a Guggenheim Fellowship. He eventually became a teacher at Frederick Douglass Junior High School in Harlem. A branch of the New York Public Library, opened in 1988 on West 136th Street as an extension of the Schomburg Center, has been dedicated to his memory.

Both of these young writers went on to write successful novels through the 1920s, and their success was matched by other black writers as well. But they weren't all singing with the same voice, and that was among the things that made the Harlem Renaissance so stimulating for all of them. Cullen and Claude McKay chose to follow traditional patterns that had been established earlier by white novelists, but, on the other hand, Hughes and some of the others believed that their mission should be mining black sources, such as jazz and the language of the streets, to produce a new and entirely different literary form.

Their endless debates and discussions at places like the 135th Street branch of the New York Public Library, which became the Schomburg Center in 1978, didn't always change their opinions, but it crystallized their thinking and it gave them a better understanding of the new ethnic pride that they were all developing. The Renaissance attracted painters, sculptors and photographers, too. And, of course, the Harlem musicians who had been there all along, provided the background music, as well as an inspiration to all of them as well as to outsiders who ventured uptown to share in the phenomenon.

The *New York Herald* gave this new culture its name when it reported that "America is on the edge . . . of what might not improperly be called a Negro renaissance," But if the movement was national in scope, its heart was in Harlem, and among the hundreds who made it happen, only the poet Countee Cullen had been raised there. All of the other writers and artists migrated to the new center of the action from every corner of the United States as well as from the Caribbean. And, although Cullen had been raised on Lenox Avenue, he had actually been born in the South, and he wasn't a native Harlemite, either. The fact was that Harlem had been a largely white community as recently as twenty years before the renaissance began. There were almost no blacks living in central Harlem before the beginning of the twentieth century.

Countee Cullen's foster father, Reverend F. A. Cullen, became one of the pioneers of black Harlem when he established the Salem Memorial Mission there in 1902. The section, which had been a farming community in the days of the Dutch settlement of New York, had grown by then into a neighborhood of well-established middle-class German Jews and second-generation families of Irish and English immigrants.

Its first spurt of growth began in the 1880s after the elevated railroads pushed that far north and offered an opportunity for Manhattanites who could afford it to get their first taste of suburban living. Many of them built imposing town houses in the uptown neighborhood, and developers jumped in to offer white families up-to-the-minute luxury apartments in buildings that had elevators, servants' quarters, and rents to match.

By the time the Lenox Avenue subway line reached 155th Street in 1904, there was virtually no vacant land left between there and the northern end of Central Park, and everybody, it seemed, from big insurance companies to housewives, was dabbling in Harlem real estate. Working people were gladly paying off mortgages as high as $75,000 for apartment buildings that were bringing in less than $5,000 a year in rents and, more often than not, they used the rental income to come up with down payments on more buildings to pyramid their profits. Then the bottom dropped out. There were more buildings in Harlem than there were people to fill them. Rents ranged up to $45 a month, higher than in most other parts of Manhattan at the turn of the century, and even when landlords began offering two or three months free for new tenants, the cost was still out of the question for the average New York family. Block after block of Harlem apartments were left standing empty.

Companies and families that had invested in Harlem property were faced with financial ruin, but some of them found a way out in the form of the blacks who were beginning to arrive from the South in huge numbers, along with local African-Americans who were being uprooted as the large all-black neighborhood in midtown was being destroyed to make way for the new Penn Station. For them, the prospect of moving to Harlem wasn't just a move uptown, but it represented a chance for a big upward step in their lifestyle.

Of course, renting apartments to blacks wasn't every landlord's cup of tea, and most Harlem property owners banded together and made pledges among themselves that would restrict their buildings to whites only, and, if they all kept their promises to each other, the blocks around them as well. But their need for rental income was too great, and when Phil Payton, a local black realtor, offered to lease entire buildings and guarantee their owners a fixed annual income, many of the restrictive covenants began to fall by the wayside. The trend he started lasted only until about 1916 when the last of the previously designated "white only" buildings had begun to open their doors to blacks. For their owners, it was their only alternative to foreclosure.

Just about every American city had a segregated black community in those days, and virtually every one of them seemed to be centered around some dark and uninviting alley where nobody else would even think of living. But there weren't any alleys anywhere in

Harlem. In fact, its major boulevard, Lenox Avenue, where the Hell-fighters ended their march in 1919, is wider than Fifth Avenue, where the parade began. All of the crosstown streets in the neighborhood were tree-lined, and so were the avenues. Nearly all of the buildings, even the tenements, were new and modern, and a large number of apartments in them had never been occupied since they were built. By any standard, Harlem was one of Manhattan's most desirable neighborhoods. For the first time in history, black families were given an opportunity to live in relative luxury.

An Urban League report published in 1914 said: "Those of the race who desire to live in grand style, with elevator, telephone and hall boy service, can now realize their cherished ambition." The rents they were forced to pay were often inflated—Phil Payton added 10 percent to the rents in the buildings he controlled—but it seemed well-worth it to a great many black families, especially considering what they were getting for their money.

The black churches that had been established for generations in places like Greenwich Village and the midtown Tenderloin neighborhood followed their parishioners up to Harlem. For the most part, they were able to finance the move by selling their former properties during what was a boom time in downtown real estate. Nearly all of them used the resulting funds to buy or build new churches uptown, and most of them had enough cash left over to buy other property in Harlem, where the real estate market was still depressed.

Chief among the newcomers was St. Philip's Episcopal Church. The parish had been given a large plot of land on West 30th Street in 1830, and it was holding the property as the future site of a cemetery when its value zoomed up from $9,000 to $450,000 virtually overnight. The parish had already sold its church building five blocks away for $140,000, and when St. Philip's made the move up to Harlem in 1909, it had become one of the richest churches any-where in the city. It was about to become wealthier still by investing in Harlem real estate.

Most of the blocks in Harlem were still controlled by white-only covenants in 1909, but the rector of St. Philip's, Reverend Hutchens Bishop, was a light-skinned man who could easily pass for white. Property owners who never thought to question his race were pleased to hear that he was interested in buying their buildings. Not only that, he was offering to pay cash for them. After buying prop-erties in his own name, Reverend Bishop simply signed the deeds over to his parish and, by 1911, it owned several dozen apartment houses close to its brand-new church building on West 134th Street. And all of them were filled with African-American tenants.

Just about every black parish that moved to Harlem followed St. Philip's lead, and together they were more instrumental in turning it into a black enclave than all of the black real estate operators put together. At the time Colonel Hayward established the 15th Regi-ment of Colored National Guard in Harlem, there were 60,534 Negroes living in Manhattan; 49,555 of them called Harlem home. By the time the regiment came home from the war four years later, two-thirds of Manhattan's black population—about 73,000 people—were concentrated in the area bounded by Fifth and Eighth avenues, and 130th and 145th streets. Over the next ten years that number grew to 164,565, and the southern boundary of black Harlem was extended a mile downtown to 110th Street along the northern edge of Central Park, while the northern boundary also pushed farther uptown along St. Nicholas Avenue into Washington Heights. Harlem had become the largest colony of black people any-where in America, if not the world, and it was the fastest-growing neighborhood in all of Manhattan. It had become the Promised Land for blacks in the Deep South, and more and more of them were beginning to make plans to move there.

In the meantime, the white population of Manhattan had dropped noticeably by 1930, after the subways were extended into the other boroughs, and new and better neighborhoods were established in them. Overall, the number of Manhattanites dropped by 18 percent during the 1920s, but at the same time, the borough's black population rose by 106 percent. And more than three-quarters of them were living in Harlem.

The Roaring Twenties also saw the emergence of a new kind of "New Negro" on Harlem's streets. They came from the West Indies, where the restrictive immigration laws of the postwar era allowed them to emigrate under quotas that had been established for British and French immigrants, whose nationality they technically shared. The law set limits on the number of people who could emigrate from specific countries, based on averages from previous decades. It was a bald attempt to curb the flow from Central European and Mediterranean countries, but because relatively few French or British nationals had been among the late-nineteenth-century Ellis Island arrivals, their quotas were almost wide open, and the only would-be Americans interested in filling them were in the Caribbean.

Unlike the Southern blacks who were also establishing themselves in Harlem at the time, the islanders generally behaved like every other immigrant group and banded together under the flag, culture, and customs of the homeland they left behind.

There was very little racial discrimination in the Caribbean islands. A man's self-worth was determined by his place in the social pecking order, which was open to everyone. That tended to make these immigrants eager to rise above the menial jobs they were forced to take at first, and many of them succeeded, which made their new neighbors resentful. As the saying went, when one of them got "ten cents above a beggar, he opened a business." Indeed, that seemed to be the case. Moreover, as a group, West Indian families tended to be more stable because they were centered around strong fathers, who made sure their families worked to become successful. This was in contrast to the descendants of American slaves where the father figure was absent more often than not, and there was no one nagging them to work themselves up beyond the poverty level.

The West Indian immigrants were also more likely to be Catholics and Episcopalians than Methodists and Baptists, as the majority of Harlemites were, and they lived by a moral code that others considered too strict to be bearable, even to watch, which helped enhance their status as outsiders. In other words, all that the native-born and immigrant Harlemites had in common was the color of their skin, and the islanders often seemed to be almost white by comparison. Summing up the situation, one prominent Harlem leader wrote that, "We have in Harlem this strange mixture of reactions not only to prejudice from without, but to equally potent prejudices from within."

The problem finally came to an end in the 1930s, when immigration began to slow down. The second generation adapted to the idea that both groups were going to have to face up to the issue of "prejudice from without," and they closed ranks. But the Harlem community had been divided at a time when overcrowding was making life tougher and more expensive for everyone, and nobody seemed willing to raise their voice in a protest that might benefit the opposite side.

The result was that while the Harlem Renaissance was bringing new life and new hope uptown, the overcrowding of the neighborhood seemed to be making it slowly deteriorate into a slum. But that represented an opportunity for some because the demand for living space brought the real estate boom back with a vengeance. By the mid–1920s, when Manhattan's population density was 223 per acre, the average was 336 in Harlem, which made it the most congested neighborhood not just in the North, but possibly anywhere in America. The sudden growth in population had created an incredible demand for living space, and landlords, black as well as white, started cashing in with higher rents. The average monthly rent for Harlem apartments doubled from $21 to $41 during the 1920s, while the typical family was earning only about $1,300 a year through the entire period.

But there did seem to be a way out of the dilemma. Most of Harlem's buildings had originally been built with affluent white tenants in mind. Most of them had large families and they usually needed extra space to house their servants as well, and so the apartments frequently had as many as seven rooms, Few black families had more than one or two children in the 1920s (according to the 1930 census, less than 18 percent of Harlemites were under fourteen years old, compared to nearly 25 percent of the overall population), and more than half of the people who were apartment-hunting at the time were still single. Even among those with larger families to house, none of them needed a seven-room apartment, especially at $70 per month But all of that extra space could be rerented to strangers, and some people signed leases hoping to sublease the extra space, maybe even bringing enough money that they themselves could live rent-free. The problem was that these lodgers were nearly always an unknown quantity, and many an amateur landlord found out the hard way that not everyone is "respectable."

Brownstone owners played the game, too. By converting their buildings into one-room "studio" apartments, owners could easily gross up to three times as much as they had before. Some of them converted their homes into rooming houses, and even rented out the bathtubs as sleeping space. Others among them rented the same space to more than one person at a time, taking advantage of the fact that many people were working on different shifts and didn't mind sharing so-called "hot beds" with other people who worked at night and slept during the day.

The situation led to a unique Harlem phenomenon called the "rent party," which the local newspaper, *The Age*, called "a recognized means of meeting the demands of extortionist landlords." Harlem families who had the space to accommodate them staged enough of these parties that it was easily possible to go to several of them any night of the week. The fun usually began at around midnight and it lasted until the sun came up. Anybody with the twenty-five-cent price of admission was welcome, and revelers could buy whiskey and wine and heaping plates of homemade coleslaw, potato salad, chitterlings, and pigs' feet, along with all of the other dishes that later became classified as "soul food." In that way, they were able to make a contribution to the monthly rent bill beyond the quarter they had paid to get through the door.

Stride piano player Willie "The Lion" Smith, a regular at Leroy's, one of the few Harlem night spots that catered exclusively to black audiences, was among many musicians who provided entertainment at rent parties after the clubs closed for the night. As he recalled the typical scene, " You would see all kinds of people making the party scene; formally-dressed society folks from downtown, policemen, painters, carpenters, mechanics, truckmen in their workingmen's clothes, gamblers, lesbians, and entertainers of all kinds. The parties were recommended to newly arrived single gals as the place to go to get acquainted."

And these parties were anything but amateur nights. The entertainers often included musicians like Fats Waller and Duke Ellington. The literati usually considered rent parties, which were called "struts," "jumps," or "shouts," beneath their dignity, but novelist Wallace Thurman, an iconoclast among them, who disdainfully characterized the others as "Niggerati," not only admitted that he frequented the parties, but he described one in his novel, *The Blacker the Berry*: " 'Ahhh, sock it.' . . . 'Ummmm' . . . Piano playing, slow, loud, discordant, accompanied by the rhythmic sound of shuffling feet. Down a long, dark hallway to an inside room, lit by a solitary red bulb. 'Oh play it, you dirty no-gooder.' . . . A room full of dancing couples, scarcely moving their feet, arms completely encircling one anothers' bodies."

If the neighbors didn't mind all-night parties in their buildings, one common complaint they all shared was that everyone's quality of life seemed to be dragged down by Southerners who had grown up in sharecroppers' cabins and had never known such conveniences as indoor plumbing or electric lights. Worse, few of them had the slightest idea how to cope with breakdowns, let alone prevent them. By and large, none of them had ever lived in a city before, and most of them didn't seem to realize that such things as tossing trash into hallways or out of windows might not be the right thing to do—or that anybody had any responsibility at all for how their neighbors lived.

Over a relatively short time, landlords began to act as though they had no responsibilities, either, except for collecting the rent, of course. In response to looted apartments and stolen fixtures, many of them simply stopped making basic repairs. If a furnace broke down, their tenants were forced to do without heat; if pipes leaked, kitchens and bathrooms flooded, and the water usually poured down into the apartment below, often taking the ceiling with it. If rats moved in, as they invariably did, tenants were left to ward them off by themselves.

Yet, for all that, almost no one living under these conditions believed that Harlem was a slum by any stretch of the imagination. Most of these new Harlemites had come from the Deep South, where self-respect was unheard-of among blacks and advancement in society was completely out of the question. More than almost anything else, the Hellfighters helped to give the citizens of Harlem a new unshakable self-confidence along with a belief that, given a chance, there was nothing that they weren't able to accomplish, just as the war had turned ordinary men into heroes that the whole country seemed to admire.

While most of the newly emerging intellectual class seemed to be determined to "tell it like it is," the stories they sometimes overlooked—but that Harlemites treasured most—were the ones about ordinary people like themselves who managed to save their money and put their kids through college, or even people in show business or the rackets who thumbed their noses at the racists. And for the most part, the stories they told and retold weren't fantasies, but were based on the experiences of real people who lived just around the corner.

Among Harlem's most admired role models was Lillian Harris, who had arrived in the city in 1901 with five dollars in her pocket. She spent three of those dollars on a baby carriage and a boiler, and the rest on pigs' feet. And then she took to the streets. The menu of her "portable restaurant" grew quickly to include hog maw, chitterlings, and corn, but she was still know as "Pig Foot Mary." By the time she moved to the corner of 135th Street and Lenox Avenue in 1917, she had long since traded the baby carriage for a portable steam table she had designed herself and she gave up the single life for the company of the man who owned a newsstand on the same corner. Together they invested in Harlem real estate, as well as property in California, where they later retired. Her investments turned Pig Foot Mary into one of Harlem's richest women. She was a tough, no-nonsense landlord, but her tenants admired her anyway because of her rags-to-riches story that they knew could be theirs, too, if only they had saved their money like she did.

William Mack Felton, another Harlem legend, arrived from Georgia with nothing but a dollar tucked into his shoe. On his first day in town, he met a pawn shop owner who had a store full of clocks that didn't work. Realizing that they just needed cleaning, Felton invested his dollar in a washtub and a gallon of kerosene. By the end of the day, all of the clocks were ticking. Then he went on to repairing watches, bicycles, guns, and anything else that appeared to be broken, but was more likely to be just dirty. When automobiles appeared on the streets of New York, Felton began repairing them, too, and then he opened a school to teach people how to drive them. True to his original calling, Felton also invented a machine to wash them and became a millionaire.

Among other Harlemites who put Horatio Alger to shame was a former laundress named Madame C. J. Walker, who made her fortune with a patented hair-straightening process and bought the first brand-new mansion built in Harlem since before the turn of the century, not to mention building an impressive villa in the Hudson River Valley just down the road from millionaire Jay Gould. Madame Walker also became active in politics, and when the War Department first announced that it was scrapping its plan to train black officers for the coming war, she personally went to Washington to let President Wilson know how she felt about that affront.

If statisticians and social reformers were writing death notices for the uptown neighborhood, though, the influence of the Harlem Renaissance was leading to the very different perception—even among most white Americans—that it was one of the most fascinating places in the entire country. Blacks everywhere in the country were sharing that opinion. When Langston Hughes first arrived there in 1921, he wrote: "I can never put on paper the thrill of the underground ride to Harlem. I went up the steps and out into the bright September sunlight. Harlem! I stood there, dropped my bags, took a deep breath and felt happy again." The poet Arna Bontemps wrote that it was only after migrating to Harlem from California, that he realized "it was fun to be Negro." He added, "In some places, the autumn of 1924 may have been an unremarkable season, but in Harlem it was like a foretaste of paradise. A blue haze descended at night and with it strings of fairy lights on the broad avenues."

The autumn of 1924 was a significant date for the Hellfighters, too. It was when they finally got an armory of their own, a combination of medieval and Art Deco architecture designed by the firm of Tachau & Vought, overlooking the Harlem River at the northern end of Fifth Avenue on the corner of 143rd Street. After its adjoining administration building was added in 1933, it was the biggest and the most impressive National Guard armory anywhere in New York State. Certainly, the regiment's war record had everything to do with it, but it was the attention that the Harlem Renaissance was creating that helped cut through the red tape to speed up the project. It was built in less time than it had taken Colonel Hayward to get rifles for his men back in 1915, when he was building the regiment itself.

During that same year, Harlem Hospital started admitting black doctors to its staff and opened a new school for nurses. The institution also began accepting applications from black medical students to serve their internships there. Harlem was clearly on a roll.

The community was becoming all that W. E. B. Du Bois had hoped it would grow into, a magnet for the most gifted men and women of the Negro race. The best part was that it wasn't going unnoticed, although sometimes for the wrong reasons. People were beginning to think of Harlem as "the Paris of America," where downtown "swells" filled nightclubs and cabarets, speakeasies and dance clubs night after night to listen to jazz, dance the Charleston and be entertained by "exotic" singers and dancers. They called it "slumming," but few of them had any idea how ironic that was. What they were enjoying was the nonstop excitement of Harlem's nightlife, and most of them never saw the daytime reality which, hopefulness aside, was every bit as different as night and day.

A great deal of Harlem's after-dark pleasures were reserved for whites only. Both the Cotton Club and Connie's Inn, each of which claimed to have the hottest shows in town, closed their doors to black customers, although their prices would probably have made the restriction unnecessary. But along with all the other nightspots the Jazz Age spawned, both of them owed their style to Happy Rhone's, which encouraged the races to mingle. Rhone was the first to present floor shows anywhere in New York, and the Hellfighter's former drum major, Noble Sissle, was his most frequent master of ceremonies. Rhone's was often called the "millionaire's club," but its prices were still low enough to allow Harlem's middle class to associate with such well-heeled "swells" as John Barrymore and Charlie Chaplin. Other celebrities like them could often also be found in the block of 133rd Street off Lenox Avenue that was called "The Jungle," where places like the Bucket of Blood and Basement Brownie's were doing a turn-away business night after night.

For the most part, the local writers and poets gathered at Small's Paradise on 135th Street, a few steps away from the YMCA where several of them lived, and all of them gathered for lectures, discussions, and plays. The "Y" became legendary among black theatrical hopefuls when Paul Robeson landed the lead in Eugene O'Neill's play *The Emperor Jones* after producers from the Provincetown Playhouse discovered him on the YMCA stage. Although there is no record of lightning ever having struck twice there, every actor in productions staged at the "Y" from that moment on performed as though it might happen at any moment.

The new intellectuals could also find stimulation at concerts by the Harlem Symphony, a realization of Jim Europe's fondest dream that was finally brought together by Fletcher Henderson. Harlem also had a string quartet of its own in the '20s, and its performances were always very well attended. There were also several "salons" where invited guests assembled to discuss art, literature, poetry, and politics virtually every night of the week.

It was an extension of nightly gatherings of intellectuals that was started in Paris by poet and arts patron Gertrude Stein and was brought to New York during the First World War by one of her disciples, Mabel Dodge, who gathered writers and artists together in her Greenwich Village apartment and set the tone for the Village's "Bohemian" movement of the 1920s. Harlem writers and artists frequently took the subway downtown to join in the discussions, which were expanded to dozens of Village saloons and coffee shops, but it wasn't long before wealthy Harlemites began to open their doors to them so that they could find stimulation closer to home.

The salons, parties, and soirees attracted white philanthropists as well as the local intellectuals. Guest lists often included Rockefellers, Villards, Stokeses, and du Ponts, all of whom were eager to put their money to work helping Harlem pull itself up by its own bootstraps. They provided the funds to establish schools and build new housing; they financed new businesses and they kept organizations like the NAACP and the Urban League alive.

The social affairs also brought publishers and show-business entrepreneurs into the community in search of new talent, and their forays usually paid off on both sides of the table. As Langston Hughes described it:

> It was a period when, at almost every Harlem upper-crust dance or party, one would be introduced to various white celebrities there as guests. It was a period when almost any Harlem Negro of any social importance at all would be likely to say casually, "As I was remarking the other day to Heywood . . . " meaning [newspaper columnist] Heywood Broun. Or, "'As I said to George . . . " referring to [composer] George

Gershwin. It was a period when local and visiting royalty were not at all uncommon in Harlem.

The Harlem Renaissance produced twenty-six novels, ten books of poetry, and literally hundreds of short stories, as well as five Broadway plays, a few ballets, and several classical music compositions as well as a large body of paintings and sculpture. Although hundreds of creative people made Harlem their headquarters in the '20s, the success of the renaissance actually came through the output of only about a half-dozen of them. And the man who kept it all moving forward was Charles Johnson, who had started the movement in the first place. One of his most important discoveries was not a writer or an artist, but a historian named Arthur Schomburg, whom he called on to ". . . enrich us with a mite of your immense knowledge of our subject."

Schomburg was born in San Juan, Puerto Rico, and was educated in Santurce, Puerto Rico, and St. Croix, U.S. Virgin Islands. After migrating to Harlem in 1891 he became active in the cause of Puerto Rican and Cuban independence. He was elected secretary and treasurer of the Negro Society for Historical Research and founded the Negro Book Exchange. By the time the Harlem Renaissance began, he had already put together one of the world's largest collections of books, pamphlets, prints, and paintings related to black history. He sold it all to the New York Public Library in 1926 and in 1932 became the collection's chief curator until his death in 1938. It became officially known as the Schomburg Center for Research in Black Culture in 1972. During the years of the renaissance, Schomburg served as the movement's eyes and ears in the community, as well as its authority on all that had gone on before.

If the Harlem Renaissance had its resident historian, it also had its official tour guides in Ethel Nance and her roommates, Regina Anderson and Louella Tucker. Newcomers were directed to their apartment near Sugar Hill at 580 St. Nicholas Avenue by the Urban League. Once there they could count on getting a meal and a place to sleep for a night or two while the women introduced them to the neighborhood. They also checked out their credentials and then began introducing them to people who could help them in their careers. Not everybody made the cut, but it was a necessary first step for anyone who wanted to make something of their talents in the Harlem of the 1920s.

Not everybody needed a special invitation to show off their talents in Harlem in those days. One spot that stood out above all the others was the Savoy Ballroom, which opened on Lenox Avenue and 140th Street—just for the sheer joy of it—in 1926. It was made famous by Edgar Sampson's classic "Stompin' at the Savoy," written eight years later. Many of the former members of the 369th Regiment Band, and quite a few veterans of Jim Europe's Clef Club Orchestra were regular performers there. In fact, had Jim Europe lived, he would probably have found a permanent home at the Savoy. Instead, the baton was wielded by Fletcher Henderson, the man who had picked up where Jim had left off and transformed big ragtime bands into big jazz bands.

Unlike Jim Europe, Henderson had the advantage of being able to reach a national audience through radio, and regular broadcasts of his Savoy jam sessions turned jazz into a coast-to-coast craze. Purists among jazz historians argue that the best sounds were coming out of Chicago and New Orleans back then; but if musicians like King Oliver and Kid Ory, Louis Armstrong and Bobby Williams were better, their audiences were smaller and they eventually had to take their horns to Harlem.

The intellectuals usually looked down their noses at the new sounds. As far as they were concerned, it was the music of speakeasies, brothels, and rent parties, and an insult to the race. But most of them were willing to make an exception in the case of the sounds that were coming out of the Savoy. They were practically irresistible.

Henderson had been a recording manager for the Black Swan Recording Company ("The Only Genuine Colored Record—Others are Only Passing for Colored"), which scored a big hit in 1922 with a single by Trixie Smith, a blues singer who had won the 369th Infantry Regimental Band's first concert competition the previous year. But Ethel Waters was an even bigger moneymaker for the label, as was Henderson's band itself. It was the recording studios as much as the radio broadcast booths that eventually lured the best jazz musicians to Harlem. But when they got there, they sometimes found themselves upstaged by giants like Duke Ellington and Cab Calloway, not to mention Paul Whiteman, whose orchestra was beginning to sound more and more like Fletcher Henderson's every day.

The beat went on right up through the end of the decade and beyond, but the momentum of the Harlem Renaissance began showing signs of slowing down in the early 1930s, when the literati found a new cause in the form of communism, which Countee Cullen announced " . . . alone is working to educate and organize the classes dispossessed by the present system." Langston Hughes went him one better by endorsing the candidacy of William Z. Foster, the Communist party's presidential hopeful in the 1932 campaign, and his black running mate, James W. Ford.

The Great Depression had hit the country by then, and many of Harlem's glittering nightclubs folded. A few of them were recycled as churches. And for all the hope and hoopla that the renaissance had produced, most black families were no better off than they were when it all began. Rents were still out of sight, and most jobs with any kind of future were still closed to blacks. There were still high hopes in the black community that Franklin D. Roosevelt's promised "New Deal" was going to come to their rescue, but when the programs were actually enacted, blacks were excluded from most of the jobs they created, and they were usually paid lower salaries if they were lucky enough to land a job.

The NAACP had been pushing for federal antilynching laws since 1919, but it never managed to succeed in getting legislation passed. During his presidential campaign, Roosevelt declared that the time had come for such legislation, but when push came to shove, he was forced to send a message to civil rights leaders that congressional leaders were opposing him: "They will block every bill I ask Congress [to pass] to keep America from collapsing. I just can't take that risk." After all these years, from the 369th Regiment's sacrifice in war to Roosevelt's New Deal, almost nothing at all had really changed as far as black America was concerned.

As one disillusioned leader said of the Harlem Renaissance, "the sympathies of the intellectuals have been with the few who exploit this word for the good of the few."

The movement that had begun as an antidote to urban riots ended with an outbreak of major proportions in Harlem on the night of March 19, 1935. A teenager had been beaten by clerks in a store where he had been accused of stealing a pocketknife, and rumors started spreading through the community that he had been beaten to death. Apparently led by militants from the Young Communist League, an estimated ten thousand Harlemites took to the streets and went on a rampage, destroying some $2 million worth of white-owned property. By the time the sun came up the next morning, three of them were dead, more than a hundred were behind bars, and thirty were in the hospital. The sun had finally set on the Harlem Renaissance.

The 369th Regiment of the New York National Guard, which had been instrumental in starting the ball rolling with its message of black pride, officiated over the movement's funeral. Its men were the ones who were called out to put down the riot that night, almost exactly sixteen years after they had marched up Lenox Avenue in triumph.

PART 2
OTHER TIMES, OTHER HEROES

7

A New War to Fight

By the mid–1930s, Colonel Hayward's hopes were finally realized when the 369th Regiment became the first Negro National Guard outfit with an all-black officer corps. Its commanding officer was Colonel Benjamin O. Davis, Sr., who later made history when he became the first African-American general ever to serve in the U.S. Army.

Davis had been a "temporary" first lieutenant in the Eighth Infantry during the Spanish-American War in 1898, and he was mustered out after the war was over. He applied for admission to the U.S. Military Academy at West Point soon afterward, but when his application was turned down—a routine occurrence among black candidates—he decided to take a different route to a commission, and enlisted as a private in the Ninth Cavalry. He rose quickly through the ranks and became a second lieutenant in less than a year. His first posting as a commissioned officer was in the Philippines. Then, after having served stateside as a professor of military science and tactics at Wilberforce University in Ohio, and then in Liberia as military attaché at the U.S. Embassy in Monrovia, he was sent back to the Philippines again, where he was forced to sit out the First World War.

Before Colonel Davis arrived in New York to take command of the 369th, he had seen service as a military science professor at the Tuskegee Institute in Alabama, and he had commanded a cavalry regiment that was assigned to patrolling the Mexican border in Arizona. His service as the ranking officer of the Hellfighters lasted from 1938 through 1941, when he was reassigned as brigade commander of the Second Cavalry Division. But before he left New York, Davis had contributed another chapter to the history of the Hellfighters with his promotion to the rank of brigadier general in the regular army.

By the time World War II began, the army had exactly five black senior officers. Three of them were chaplains; the other two were named Davis.

General Davis's son, Benjamin O. Davis, Jr., who himself would eventually become the first African-American four-star general in the U.S. Air Force, graduated from the U.S. Military Academy in 1936, which gave him the distinction of becoming the first black West Point graduate in nearly fifty years, and only the fourth in the academy's history. But although he finished thirty-fifth out of 276 in his class, his fellow cadets seemed determined to make sure that he wouldn't finish at all.

His first clue that it was going to be a rough ride came on the first day when he was assigned a room to himself, while all of the other plebes either doubled or tripled up. He realized that he was in for big trouble a month later when he stumbled on a meeting of his classmates that had been called to discuss "what to do about the nigger." What they decided to do was ignore him, and for the next four years, nobody talked to Cadet Davis except when duty required it. He ate alone, exercised alone, and in the dance classes that were required of every cadet, he danced alone, wandering aimlessly around the floor without a partner. When the class was taken to football games and other off-campus events, he had a bus all to himself.

Looking back on the experience, he wrote: "West Point is supposed to train leaders, but there was no damn leadership at all. . . . The first captain of cadets was William Westmoreland [the future U.S. commander in Vietnam]. If he'd been a true leader, he would have stopped that crap. It was designed to make me buckle, but I refused to buckle. They didn't understand that I was going to stay there, and I was going to graduate. I was not missing anything by not associating with them. They were missing a great deal by not knowing me." Months later, one of his classmates broke the silence with a letter to him: "The narrow-mindedness of some people is astounding and I believe that this place, instead of diminishing that quality in men, increases it."

A week after Davis graduated, he was married in the West Point chapel, but there was no rush from the door under an arch of crossed swords, as is traditional at every academy wedding. There were no guests except the bride and groom's families.

The newly commissioned Lieutenant Davis was assigned to the infantry school at Fort Benning, Georgia, where the silent treatment continued. This time it extended to his wife, Agatha. When they made the obligatory courtesy call on the post commandant, nobody answered the door, and when he tried to join the officers' club, his application was denied. ("You won't be using it," said the rejection note.)

His excellent academic record at the Point, where he ranked thirty-fifth in his class of 276, entitled Davis to choose any branch of the army. After his short stint at Benning, he picked the air corps. He had learned to fly during his student days, but that didn't seem to matter. His request was turned down because there weren't any black flying units available, and it was against army policy to assign black officers to positions where they might outrank white junior officers. Or, for that matter, to give orders to white enlisted men.

Instead, Davis was assigned to ROTC training at Tuskegee Institute, an assignment he characterized as a "useless existence." "What happens to these men after they are trained?" he asked. And then he answered his own question: "They are given duties as servants in officers' quarters. They had no combat mission." Almost twenty years after Henry Johnson, Needham Roberts, and the Hellfighters of Harlem had turned in a glorious battlefield record, black soldiers were still considered unfit for combat.

During the years between the wars, the military dithered over the role of blacks in their ranks and conducted endless studies that all came to the same conclusion: Negroes weren't qualified for anything but menial jobs under close supervision. One of the War Department's surveys, conducted in response to an NAACP demand for black recruitment into the air corps, proved, to the military's satisfaction, at least, "The colored man has not been attracted to flying in the same way or to the extent of the white man." Case closed.

Their research overlooked the fact that several aviation pioneers had been black men and women. There were a dozen or so black barnstormers stunt-flying around the country even as the study was being made, and some of them had already flown the coast-to-coast round trip, back when it took two weeks just to fly one way. Few others, blacks or whites, were even interested in the idea of giving it a try. The first black pilot to cross the country was Cal Rogers, who did it in forty-nine days back in 1911, only eight years after the Wright brothers flew for the first time.

Strangely, none of the researchers seemed to have heard anything about Herbert Fauntleroy Julian, the "Black Eagle of Harlem," who began his flying career in 1924. He was hard to miss. When he was on the ground, Julian always wore a morning coat with tails, striped formal trousers, and spats. He had a thin mustache, and he wore a monocle and a derby hat. When he was flying, he wore riding breeches and knee-length boots, and when he appeared at air shows, he was driven to his plane in a black LaSalle touring car with its top down.

Julian's signature stunt was parachuting out of the plane playing a saxophone. He was, in fact, the first pilot to make a parachute drop over Manhattan, although he was arrested for his trouble. He also attempted the first solo flight from New York to Africa; but after taking off with great ceremony from the Harlem River in a seaplane, he never made it any further than Flushing Bay, where he crashed.

Things began to change in 1939 when the Civil Aeronautics Administration started its Civilian Pilot Training Program (CPT), to build up a reserve of trained fliers in case of a national emergency. At first the program was limited to students at all-white colleges, but aviation pioneer Chauncy Spencer, another of those African-American wing-walking stunt fliers that the military researchers missed, flew activist Edgar Brown from Chicago to Washington to lobby the Military Appropriations Committee to expand the CPT program to include blacks as well. The first person they met there was Senator (and future President) Harry Truman, who seemed incredulous when they told him that even through they were taxpaying American citizens, they weren't allowed to join the air corps. Truman promised them, "We'll see that it doesn't happen again."

True to his word, he convinced the committee to extend the program to include the campuses of six black colleges, and two years later, in 1941, the Army Air Corps agreed to start recruiting the CPT's black graduates into the newly formed 66th Pursuit Squadron. When Air Corps commander General Henry "Hap" Arnold, signed off on the idea, he specified that the squadron would be "experimental," and he made it clear that if the experiment didn't work, he expected the squadron to be dismantled. He also confided to his superiors that since it was out of the question for black pilots to give orders to white mechanics and ground crews—and he was fairly certain that it could take as many as ten years to train blacks for those jobs—the whole idea was probably doomed from the start anyway.

It was also "common knowledge" that black people couldn't handle an airplane, but that myth was put to rest in 1941 when First Lady Eleanor Roosevelt was invited to watch maneuvers by the men of the 66th. When she met Charles Anderson, the chief instructor (who had earned his commercial pilot's license back in 1933), she commented, "I always heard the colored can't fly an airplane. But everybody here is flying, so that must not be the case. As a matter of fact, I'm going to find out for myself and take a flight with you."

At first, the Secret Service refused to let her do such a foolish thing, but, when one of them called the White House for permission, according to that part of the story, which may be apocryphal, the President himself got on the phone and said, "If Eleanor wants to fly, she's going to fly. There isn't anything any of us can do to stop her." The next thing anybody knew, Anderson was giving a command performance with the First Lady of the United States smiling in the seat behind him. It was that flight that changed an experimental program into a squadron that began calling itself the Black Eagles.

The headquarters of the new outfit was established at Tuskegee, Alabama, on the campus of the school that had been founded in 1881 by Booker T. Washington for training teachers. Although many black leaders criticized the move as just one more example of racial segregation, Tuskegee was chosen specifically because it was a black institution where segregation would insulate the men so that none of them would wash out simply because of their race. Most of the early recruits came from the CPT program, and all of them were selected following the same strict rules for qualifying every future air corps pilot. But there was one small problem. A commanding officer would have to be qualified before the program could get up and running.

Fortunately, someone remembered young Benjamin Davis, who had asked to be part of the air service, but had been turned down, and he became the first of the Tuskegee Airmen. But he came close to being turned down again.

When Davis showed up for his preflight physical, the doctor rejected him, claiming that he had detected symptoms of epilepsy. Fortunately, the air corps brass, who had often used ploys like that themselves to disqualify black officer candidates, called for a second opinion, and a few days later a different doctor gave Davis a clean bill of health and a ticket to the job that he had wanted, and had clearly merited, all along.

The 66th was formed as a pursuit squadron because the fighter planes they would fly were handled by a single person, and if the pilots were to be trained to fly larger aircraft, such as bombers, other crew members would have to be trained along with them. As it was, the required black ground crews needed 400 men to keep the squadron's twenty-seven airplanes flying, and there were thirty-three would-be pilots waiting to earn their wings,

Pilot training took eight months, and in early March 1941, five men were commissioned as lieutenants under the command of new Captain Benjamin O. Davis, Jr., who was known to all of them as "B.O.," and was regarded among his men with mixed feelings of awe and respect. All of them agreed that he was a tough CO; but, as one of them said later, "It was because of the discipline he exacted that we were able to make the record we did."

If anything, the Tuskegee program was too successful. It was turning out more black pilots than the air service had bargained for when the program was instituted, and the brass wasn't at all sure what to do with them. They were combined with three other squadrons to form the 332nd Fighter Group, and they were all activated together by the middle of 1942. But there were no marching orders to go with the activation. As white outfits were flying off to fight the war, the Tuskegee Airmen stayed where they were. There was nothing for them to do but keep on training. In the process, they built up more flying hours than any of the other pilots in the air corps. But all of those hours were spent in the skies over Alabama rather than over the battlefields of Europe or the islands in the Pacific.

Their orders finally came through in March 1943, and they were sent to Casablanca, Morocco, not long after the Germans had been driven out and the Allies were getting ready to take the war across the Mediterranean into Sicily and Italy. As was probably to be expected, they were segregated from the other units in the area, and were sent to a flying field near Fez that had only recently been a base for the German Luftwaffe. Their first assignment was to clear out the wrecked German planes that were littering the place. It seemed as though history was repeating itself as they followed the pattern that the Hellfighters found when they first landed on foreign shores and were assigned to work details, rather than combat duty

This time, though, unlike the fate of the Hellfighters, they were going to serve under their own country's flag, and not another's, and they were equipped with P-40s, the best fighter planes in the American arsenal at the time. They got their first taste of combat over Sicily a short time later in a mission to soften up enemy defenses. By July, one of the 66th's pilots, Buster Hall, had earned himself a Distinguished Flying Cross. But because the P-40 was a short-range aircraft, the squadron saw very little action during those first months, and its lack of "kills," downed enemy planes, led to a rash of "I told you so" memos back in Washington, and that led General Arnold to issue an order that the 66th Pursuit Squadron ought to be barred from combat because of its incompetence. As far as he was concerned, the Tuskegee experiment had failed, just as he had predicted it would.

B. O. Davis, whose promotion to colonel made him the highest-ranking black officer in the air corps, was called home to formally take command of the 332nd Fighter Group, but his mission turned out to be defending the 66th Squadron in congressional hearings. When the hearings ended, he had not only succeeded in saving the Tuskegee pilots, but he also managed to convince the committee that it should approve the formation of yet another all-black flying unit, the 477th Bomber Group.

While Davis was away, the 66th had been integrated into the all-white 79th Fighter Group, and it was finally seeing action flying almost fifty sorties a day. Their new unit provided the first proof that air power could be the key to establishing beachheads when it softened up the Anzio shore for the Eighth Army's invasion of Italy itself. In two weeks of action, the men of the former 66th downed twenty-four enemy planes, a new record for any American pursuit squadron. It also earned them an official commendation from no less a person than General Arnold, the man who had only recently rated them as "incompetent."

Colonel Davis arrived back in Italy after the 332nd Fighter Group was attached to the Eighth Air Force. Its bombers needed fighter support, but white pilots had developed the habit of drifting away from escort duty for dogfights where they could score more kills, and Davis's men were brought up with orders to concentrate on defense rather than offense. Although escort duty was considered beneath the dignity of all fighter pilots, black as well as white, Davis warned his pilots that he would court-martial any one of them who left bombers unprotected.

The pilots of the 332nd did as they were told. They were flying the more advanced P-51 Mustangs by then, and the African-American pilots had their planes' tails painted red so that enemy fighters could find them, although the Germans learned the hard way that it was better to avoid them, just as their fathers had learned when they met the Hellfighters in France during the last war. During the two-month air war over Italy early in 1945, the Red Tails shot down 111 enemy planes and destroyed another 150 on the ground. They flew 1,578 combat missions, more than any other squadron serving in Europe at the time. Before the fighting finally ended, eighty-eight of the Tuskegee Airmen had won the Distinguished Flying Cross and the 332nd Fighter Group itself earned a Presidential Unit Citation. Its commanding officer, Benjamin O. Davis, Jr., the son of a Hellfighter, flew sixty missions himself and won a Silver Star, the Distinguished Flying Cross, and an Air Medal with four oak leaf clusters. He also earned three Legion of Merit awards.

There was also a former Harlem Hellfighter flying with those men.

Lee Archer, whose claim of having shot down five enemy planes makes him the only black ace to have flown in World War II, first joined the army in New York as a member of 369th National Guard Regiment. The unit was being reorganized as an antiaircraft regiment at the time, but Archer was much more interested in flying airplanes than shooting them down.

When he took the air corps qualifying examination, he outscored all the other college students who took the test along with him, but they were accepted to flight school and he was not. Archer went back and took the test twice more, each time earning still higher scores than before, and he probably would have gone back for more if an officer hadn't told him the facts of life. There were no blacks in the Army Air Corps, and it was a pretty good bet that there probably never would be.

Archer transferred out of the 369th and became an instructor in an infantry training battalion. When the Tuskegee program was announced, he showed up for the test and became part of the first wave of cadets, with the highest test score of any of them. And why not? He had already aced that test three times before. As soon his training ended, Archer was promoted to captain, the first from within the cadet corps, where he had already earned a reputation as the best student on campus. He was also considered the best military person in the squadron, but that shouldn't have surprised anyone, Lee Archer had first trained among the men of the 369th, who took special pride in such accomplishments.

While Archer was going through flight training in 1941, his old outfit was called up for service with the regular army as the 369th Coast Artillery (antiaircraft) Regiment. By June 1942, it had been sent to Hawaii, where it became part of the defenses of Pearl Harbor. The regiment stayed there for two years before two of its battalions were assigned to combat duty with the Tenth Army in the Solomon Islands.

Although there had been heavy fighting in the area, especially on the islands of Okinawa and Bougainville, there were only scattered pockets of resistance to deal with by then, and getting rid of one of them became the Hellfighters' only combat engagement of the Second World War. They gave a good account of themselves, killing 63 of the enemy and capturing more than 175 of them. They also rescued 350 native civilians whom the Japanese had conscripted before the first attacks in the area and were using as slave labor to build and maintain their defenses. In the fight to capture a fortified hill, the Hellfighters destroyed several pillboxes, machine-gun nests, and mortar emplacements as well as an ammunition dump. The toll on the two battalions was only three men killed and nine wounded.

Pearl Harbor, where the rest of the regiment was based right up until the end of the war, was where it had all begun on December 7,

1941, the day Dorie Miller became the first black sailor to win the Navy Cross.

Miller was a messman aboard the battleship *West Virginia*, and he was busy with breakfast chores when the bombs started falling that morning. His ship had taken three torpedo hits and was already listing badly when a bomber scored a direct hit and she was engulfed in flames. Miller was up on deck when the bomb hit and he rushed to the bridge, where the ship's captain had been hit by shrapnel. He carried the captain off the ship and then he went back aboard to man an antiaircraft gun. Although, in accordance with navy regulations, Miller had never been trained how to use the gun, he seemed to have caught on quickly. He brought down four of the attacking planes before he ran out of ammunition and was forced to abandon ship as it was sinking.

Dorie Miller remained a messman until he was killed in action a year later. It was the only job that was available to a black man in the navy for most of the war. Despite the example of black soldiers in World War I, the military had closed ranks and intensified its segregation policies during the years between the wars, although some of the walls began to crumble when the services found themselves faced with a manpower shortage during the early months of World War II. After having resisted integration for 167 years, the U.S. Marine Corps started to accept a limited number of black volunteers in June 1942. U.S. Coast Guard had changed its policy a month earlier and, by fall, the navy agreed to accept blacks in its construction battalions, the SeaBees. The army, of course, had been accepting black volunteers all along.

Then, at the end of 1942, all of the services stopped accepting volunteers of any race. They were forced to recruit through the draft, and the Selective Service Act was quite specific that discrim-

Below: THE OFFICERS OF THE 369TH WERE TRANSFERRED TO OTHER AFRICAN-AMERICAN REGIMENTS DURING THE WAR, BUT THEY REJOINED THEIR OLD UNIT IN TIME FOR ITS HOME-COMING. LIEUTENANT COLONEL OTIS B. DUNCAN (CENTER) WAS THE HIGHEST-RANKING NEGRO TO SERVE IN WORLD WAR I. MAJOR J.R. WHITE (LEFT), AND LIEUTENANT W.J. WARFIELD (RIGHT) WERE REUNITED WITH HIM IN NEW YORK.

Above: THE HELLFIGHTERS BROUGHT A NEW KIND OF PRIDE BACK TO HARLEM FROM THE TRENCHES IN FRANCE, WHERE THEY HAD SERVED FOR 191 STRAIGHT DAYS — LONGER THAN ANY OTHER AMERICAN REGIMENT.

THE MEN OF THE 369TH SWITCHED TO FRENCH-STYLE HELMETS FROM THE FLATTER, BROADER STYLE WORN BY OTHER AMERICAN TROOPS DURING WORLD WAR I. ALTHOUGH THEY WERE OFFICIALLY AND SARTORIALLY A UNIT OF THE FRENCH ARMY, THEY WERE STILL VERY MUCH AN ALL-AMERICAN OUTFIT.

Above: THE REGIMENT'S BAND SEEMED TO NEVER STOP PLAYING, AND THEIR LEADER, JAMES REESE EUROPE PUT THEM THROUGH THEIR PACES ENTERTAINING THE TROOPS AS THEY SAILED BACK HOME FROM FRANCE.

Above: WHEN THE FIFTH AVENUE PARADE REACHED HARLEM, THE BAND STRUCK UP A RAGTIME VERSION OF "HERE COMES MY DADDY." THESE YOUNGSTERS GATHERED ALONG THE LINE OF MARCH KNEW THAT THEIR DADDIES WERE BACK HOME.

Above: ALL OF FRANCE FELL IN LOVE WITH THE 369TH'S REGIMENTAL BAND, WHICH SERENADED THE RESIDENTS OF JUST ABOUT EVERY TOWN THEY PASSED THROUGH WITH ROUSING OUTDOOR CONCERTS.

Right: THE 369TH WAS THE ONLY REGI-MENT THAT CARRIED ITS STATE FLAG THROUGHOUT THE WAR, AND THEY PROUDLY WAVED THE FLAG OF THE EMPIRE STATE AS THEY WALKED UP FIFTH AVENUE ON THE DAY THEY ARRIVED HOME.

Right: AMONG THE DIGNITARIES ON THE OFFICIAL REVIEWING STAND FOR THE 369TH'S TRIUMPHAL MARCH WERE NEW YORK'S GOVERNOR AL SMITH, AND FORMER GOVERNOR CHARLES WHITMAN WHO HAD APPROVED THE FORMATION OF THE REGIMENT. OTHERS INCLUDED NEWSPAPER TYCOON WILLIAM RANDOLPH HEARST, AND DEPARTMENT STORE OWNER JOHN WANAMAKER. PLUS, OF COURSE, THE PROUD FAMILIES OF MANY OF THE HELLFIGHTERS.

Above: THE MEN OF THE 369TH MARCHED UP FIFTH AVENUE IN THE TIGHT FORMATION PREFERRED BY THE FRENCH ARMY. IT WAS THE FIRST TIME AMERICANS HAD SEEN ANYTHING QUITE LIKE IT.

Left: When the Hellfighters arrived back in New York, they appeared in full battle dress. The man in the foreground holding his rifle is wearing a helmet he appropriated from a German soldier.

Above: Corporal Fred McIntyre, known as the "Devil's Man," carried a picture of Germany's Kaiser Wilhelm as a lucky talisman through the war. Had he been captured, it's anybody's guess what the Germans might have made of it. But not a single man of the 369th was ever captured.

Above: Some of the families who watched the Hellfighters pass by arrived with children their fathers had never seen. The command of "eyes forward" and the quick-step marching made anything more than a smile impossible, but they would get a close-up look before the day came to an end.

Right: Of all the Hellfighters, Henry Johnson was best known as the first American to earn a Croix de Guerre, France's highest honor. He had a place of honor in the homecoming parade, standing in an open car with a bouquet of flowers in his arm and his ears ringing with shouts of heartfelt affection. After all these years, he has yet to be recognized as a hero by his own government.

Below: THE UNION LEAGUE CLUB WAS AN EARLY SUPPORTER OF BLACK NATIONAL GUARD REGIMENTS IN NEW YORK, AND SPONSORED THE 367TH "BUFFALOES" REGIMENT. THE CLUB'S OFFICERS GATHERED ON A SPECIAL REVIEWING STAND TO HONOR THE HELLFIGHTERS AS THEY MARCHED UP FIFTH AVENUE.

Left: LIEUTENANT JAMES REESE EUROPE WAS FAMOUS AS A SOCIETY ORCHESTRA LEADER BEFORE THE WAR, BUT HE ENDED HIS DAYS WITH EVEN GREATER FAME AS THE LEADER OF THE 369TH REGIMENTAL BAND, EASILY THE BEST THE ARMY HAS EVER SEEN, BEFORE OR SINCE.

Below: AS THE HOMECOMING PARADE APPROACHED LENOX AVENUE IN HARLEM, EVERY INCH OF VIEWING SPACE WAS FILLED WITH PEOPLE. THE *Times* NOTED THAT "... THE SIDEWALKS WERE PACKED [FOR BLOCKS] LIKE A SUBWAY TRAIN AT THE RUSH HOUR." IT WAS AN UNDERSTATEMENT.

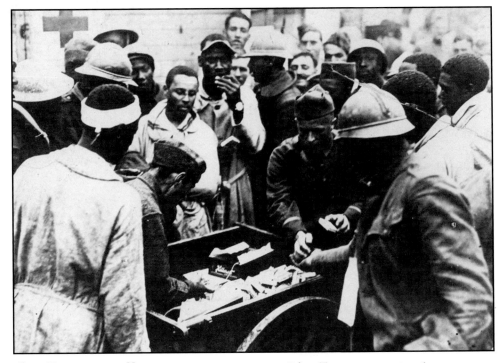

Above: TWO HUNDRED HELLFIGHTERS WERE KILLED DURING THE FIGHTING IN FRANCE, AND EIGHT HUNDRED WERE WOUNDED. THE WOUNDED WERE TRANSFERRED TO FIELD HOSPITALS BEHIND THE LINES WHERE RED CROSS UNITS KEPT THEM SUPPLIED WITH CIGARETTES, CHOCOLATE BARS AND OTHER REMINDERS OF HOME.

Below: THE MEN OF THE 369TH WENT TO FRANCE WITH A MINIMUM OF TRAINING, BUT THE FRENCH TAUGHT THEM THE ARTS OF MODERN WARFARE, INCLUDING HOW TO HANDLE A MACHINE GUN. JAMES REESE EUROPE (LEFT), THE LEADER OF THE BAND, SAW COMBAT AS THE HEAD OF A MACHINE GUN BATTALION.

Above: AFTER THEIR COUNTRY JUMPED INTO WORLD WAR I, YOUNG AFRICAN-AMERICANS FORMED LONG LINES OUTSIDE RECRUITING STATIONS WAITING FOR AN OPPORTUNITY TO GET INTO THE FIGHT. BUT, MOST ENDED UP IN WORK DETAILS INSTEAD.

Below: THE 369TH REGIMENTAL BAND DREW ITS FIRST ASSIGNMENT AT A MILITARY REST CAMP AT A POSH FORMER SPA IN THE FRENCH TOWN OF AIX LES BAINES, WHERE THEY GREETED WEARY SOLDIERS AS THEY ARRIVED BACK FROM THE FRONT AND ENTERTAINED THEM WITH MUSIC DURING THEIR STAY.

THE HELLFIGHTERS SERVED AS PART OF THE FRENCH FOURTH ARMY, UNDER GENERAL HENRI GOURAUD.

ination by race was forbidden. Like most other laws, though, there were loopholes. In practice, local draft boards generally filled requests for men on a racial quota basis rather than inducting the required numbers from the top of the eligible list. The result was that blacks were deferred with much more regularity. It was the direct opposite of the World War I experience, when blacks had been drafted in numbers well beyond their representation in the general population, despite the fact that the Army had no use for them as combat troops. In the Second World War, less than 9 percent of the men who were drafted were blacks, even though they represented almost 11 percent of the total population. In the previous war, black Americans provided almost 35 percent of all draftees, although they represented only 9 percent of the total available draft pool back then.

The 93rd Division, which included the 369th Regiment and three other activated National Guard outfits never served together as a unit during the First World War, and all four of them fought under the French flag. But the 92nd Division, which had been established to help absorb the glut of black draftees, did fight in France under American command, although the men didn't serve together as a division until the war was nearly over.

These men, known as the Buffalo Soldier Division, went into the fight in August 1918. One of its regiments, the 366th, earned a unit citation of the Distinguished Service Cross. The following month, during twenty straight days of combat, eighteen of its men earned the medal on their own. Yet the 92nd Division went home from the war under a cloud of disgrace.

During the Meuse-Argonne offensive, where they fought alongside the Hellfighters, it was charged that the some of the units of the 92nd had refused to obey orders. Although there wasn't any proof that the charge had any substance, the blame was placed on the division's black officers who were accused of "inefficiency and cowardice." Thirty of them were relieved of their command and sent home, and five of them were court-martialed for their apparent cowardice. Four were sentenced to face a firing squad and the fifth to life imprisonment. Although the sentences were eventually commuted, the stigma never left them.

During their months in France, 1,543 of the men of the 92nd Division gave their lives, as did 103 of their officers. They were awarded fifty-seven Distinguished Service Crosses, and two Croix de Guerres, one of which went to a medic. As they were leaving for home, General Pershing himself told them, " . . . the 92nd Division stands second to none in the record you have made since arriving in France." Of course, the general was referring to troops that served under his own command. However, other statements Pershing made seem to suggest that he would have been even prouder of the record established by the 369th after he cast them aside.

The 92nd was activated again late in 1942 and sent to Fort Huachua in Arizona for training. It was a miserable post out in the desert, but the only one available with segregated facilities big enough to handle its 25,000 men. Unfortunately, the War Department had reached the conclusion that black officers were incompetent, and that the only white officers who understood how to deal with black soldiers were men who had been brought up in the South. It was a disaster waiting to happen. After an inspection tour of Huachuca, General Benjamin Davis, Sr., reported: "The human element [has been] overlooked in the training of the 92nd Division. Great stress has been placed upon the mechanical perfection in execution of training missions and not enough consideration given to maintenance of racial understanding between white and colored officers and men." He might also have added that the men of 92nd universally despised their own commanding officer, who happened to hail from Virginia, and apparently didn't have the slightest idea what racial understanding meant.

The chickens came home to roost, when the men of the 92nd went into battle against crack German troops in Italy and were stopped dead in their tracks. Some of the black soldiers retreated without orders, and once again charges of "cowardice" filled stateside newspapers. By then, though, once they had that first battle under their belts, the 92nd was giving a good account of itself, But none of the folks back home were willing to give any credit to the outfit that *Newsweek* had called "a disappointment and failure." Had they been watching the division's progress through the rest of the war, they'd have know that the men of the 92nd won more than twelve thousand individual decorations, and lost one-quarter of their buddies through casualties. Still, General Mark Clark, the commander of the Fifth Army, called it "the worst division in Europe."

Most of the rest of the army brass considered it a confirmation of the ideas they had been harboring all along which they regarded as practical and not racist. As if to prove it, they shipped the black Second Cavalry Division to North Africa with a vague promise that they would soon be allowed to go into combat, although many in the War Department had already gone on record with the belief that cavalry units were obsolete and that, white or black, they were unfit to fight in a modern war like this one. As soon as they got overseas, the men of the Second were quietly transformed into stevedores.

When that news reached Washington, New York's Republican Congressman Hamilton Fish, who had seen it all before as a white officer in the 369th Regiment back in 1918, made a speech in Congress reminding his colleagues of the accomplishments of the Hellfighters. Then he said, " . . . Why, after twenty-six years of improved education for African-Americans, do we still believe that black men cannot master modern weapons? The Secretary of War is still making that accusation."

Since the 1944 presidential election was just around the corner, the White House decided to head off any more Republican criticism and ordered the all-black 93rd Infantry Division to the Pacific. Like the stories that plagued their fellows in the 92nd in Europe, rumors began to fly that the men had broken under fire. And although the majority of the men gave a good account of themselves in the jungles of Bougainville and Okinawa, their achievements went unnoticed in Washington.

The 24th Regiment, for instance, fought for five straight months without letup and captured or killed 725 Japanese troops, but it took months more for the War Department to approve a Combat Infantryman's Badge for them. The newspapers, newsreels, and news magazines took almost no notice at all. But at least there was no official criticism. In fact, General Douglas MacArthur grudgingly admitted that the blacks' contribution had been "positive."

Even though white America had turned its back on its black troops, and an army staff memorandum had stated flatly that " . . . there is a consensus that colored units are inferior to the performance of white troops, except for service duties," there were a great many exceptions to the assumption.

Among them was the 761st Tank Battalion, the first all-black armored unit in the U.S. Army. It was activated in 1942 but, like the Tuskegee airmen, it became a force without a mission, and because it was technically available to any division that needed its support, it was usually called the "Bastard Outfit," because no commander in the field seemed to think he needed them. The situation changed near the end of 1944 when Third Army commander General George S. Patton called for "the best tank battalion left in the United States," and the 761st landed at his doorstep. They went ashore on Normandy Beach in France, four months, almost to the day, after the Allied landing there on D day. Before then, Patton had refused several offers of the battalions' services on grounds that he didn't believe any black man could deal with the complicated machinery that made the thirty-five-ton Sherman tank such an incredible weapon. But his army had lost so many of the tanks and their crews by then, he was desperate for replacements. He had been given reports on the maneuvers of three black armored battalions, and picked the 761st as the best of them. In his send-off, he told the men that he didn't care what color they were, as long as they were willing to shoot " . . . every damn thing you see—little children, old ladies, everybody you see." These men knew very well what Patton thought of blacks as tankers, and his pep talk didn't have much impact on them until he ended it by telling them how much he wanted them to make a liar out of him.

They did as they were told, although they didn't mow down any children or old ladies in their path. They almost made it look easy as they led Patton's armies across France, but after their first engagement they were split up and attached to other divisions. Like other black troops, they didn't always get credit for the things they accomplished.

One example—a controversy that hasn't been settled to this day—is whether black tankers were part of the unit that liberated the Nazi concentration camp at Buchenwald in April 1945. The official version is that there no black soldiers within miles of the place, but Nobel laureate Elie Wiesel, who was among the Buchenwald survivors, wrote in the *New York Times*: "I will always remember with love a big black soldier. He was crying like a child—tears of all the pain in the world and all the rage." In spite of Wiesel's eyewitness memory, there were no black soldiers to be seen in the camp when press photographers arrived there two days later. We'll never know whether they had been quietly removed to reinforce the army's public statements that blacks weren't fit for combat or whether the camp's survivors were mistaken.

The brass never did acknowledge that without the 761st, it might have taken weeks to punch a hole through the tank traps in the impregnable Siegfried Line. The black tankers accomplished it in less than three days. That opened the door for an attack on Germany itself. But the tankers had no sooner penetrated into the Reich than word came through that the enemy had started a last-ditch effort to turn the tide back in their favor.

Their surprise attack came as three German armies—more than 500,000 troops—took over the Ardennes Forest in eastern Belgium and northern Luxembourg. Their mission was to drive four Allied armies back to the sea and give the Nazis the upper hand in forcing a peace agreement on their own terms.

The engagement that followed, remembered as the "Battle of the Bulge," resulted in more American losses than any other encounter during all of World War II. More than 600,000 American troops went into the battle—more than fought at Gettysburg. In the end there were 81,000 casualties, including 23,554 captured and 19,000 killed during four weeks of fighting in the coldest, snowiest weather anyone in the area could remember.

When the battle started, Patton's army was diverted north to spearhead the fight, and the tankers of the 761st were right in the thick of it. Their first assignment was to take the town of Tillet, a tough German stronghold where several American units had been driven back when they tried to wipe it out. The black tankers did the job in a week with sheer dogged determination and a refusal to let the Germans frighten them into retreat. These men knew that it was up to them to prove that the War Department was mistaken when it said that black men can't fight.

The Battle of the Bulge also marked the emergence of the only integrated combat unit that was allowed to fight in the war. Faced with incredible losses, General Dwight D. Eisenhower, the commander in chief of the U.S. forces in Europe, made it possible by authorizing a call for blacks assigned to service units to volunteer for the fighting.

The opportunity was limited to privates with infantry training and to noncommissioned officers who would be willing to take a reduction in rank in order to serve, as the call put it, "fighting shoulder to shoulder to bring about victory." General Benjamin O. Davis, who wrote the new orders, said that Eisenhower's decision was "the greatest since the enactment of the Constitutional Amendments following the Emancipation."

The call was answered by 2,221 black soldiers, all of whom were thrown into the Battle of the Bulge, although not as fully integrated troops as the brass had promised when they had offered them the opportunity to "fight at the side of your white brothers." Instead, they were placed in all-black platoons under white officers. Their battlefield accomplishments impressed their "white brothers." In a poll conducted later, more than three-quarters of them, officers as well as enlisted men, said they believed that these men had proven that integration in the military was an idea whose time had come.

The reaction in Washington, on the other hand, wasn't nearly as positive. The War Department called Eisenhower on the carpet for this "violation of American racial policy." A future United States senator, Robert Byrd, wrote a letter to his congressman: " . . . never in this world will I be convinced that race mixing in any field is good. All the social 'do-gooders,' . . . the reds and the pinks . . . the disciples of Eleanor [Roosevelt] . . . the pleas by [Frank] Sinatra . . . can never alter my convictions on this question."

In his original call for volunteers, Eisenhower had promised that any man who fought as an infantryman would never be reassigned to a service unit again. But, possibly because of the firestorm in Washington over his idea, when the European war ended a few months later, the black men who had been serving with the First Infantry Division were transferred to the camps that were being set up to handle displaced persons. There were also rumors that they were going to be shipped out to the Pacific, where the war was still not over, even though they all knew that army regulations called for a thirty-day furlough for combat veterans.

The Third Army under Patton had blitzed its way across France with lightning attacks involving tanks and mechanized artillery and they burned up a lot of gas in their rush. Back during the summer, Patton's regular allotment of gasoline had been cut from 400,000 to 31,000 gallons a day, and his push was stalled. Patton was furious, and he told the higher-ups that, "My men can eat their belts, but my tanks gotta have gas." Eventually, the flow was increased, but Patton was still continually on the verge of running out of gas.

The situation became critical again as they raced off to fight in the Battle of the Bulge. When the fighting ended, the well went completely dry for the tanks of the 761st. The official explanation was that the war was just about over and their job was finished, but the tankers themselves believed the rumor that they were being denied the opportunity to be the first Americans to link up with the Russians in Austria. That honor was being reserved for all-white armored divisions instead. They managed to overturn the plan when one of their supply sergeants talked the men of a black quarter-master unit into helping them steal 30,000 gallons of gas from an airfield. It was enough to get them to Austria and to be the first to link up with the Russians, even though the accomplishment was again officially ignored, as other African-American accomplishments had so often been throughout the war.

There wasn't a single man who saw combat in Europe during last months of World War II who didn't know how much he owed to the truck companies that came together to be known the Red Ball Express, although its existence was a military secret and it operated for only eighty-two days. What some of them may not have known was that the men their lives depended on were nearly all black GIs.

The Normandy invasion on June 6, 1941 was probably the most carefully planned military operation in the history of warfare, From the initial assault on the beaches to the eventual crossing over into the German homeland on D+360 (which would have been June 1, 1945) virtually every minute had been accounted for in advance. The Rhine crossing actually took place on March 19, 1945, or, as the plan would have had it, on D+287, but there was another much more serious miscalculation in the scenario.

The advance plan had called for an oil pipeline to be established as far inland as the Seine River by D+90 and then extended in stages from there. While it was being built, the plan called for bringing fuel and lubricants ashore in five-gallon cans stowed aboard assault vehicles and were then trucked inland after the beachhead was established. The plan, called Operation Overlord, went awry when the invasion force became bogged down and didn't break through until almost the end of July. But then they blew down the door with such force that a great deal of the original plan had to be scrapped in favor of a much faster attack. The plan for the oil pipeline from Cherbourg to Paris was abandoned, too, but the front lines were still relatively nearby, and there was a comfortable reserve of 7.5 million gallons of gasoline available.

But the Germans offered lighter than expected resistance. Patton's Third Army was burning 380,00 gallons of gas a day chasing them in the general direction of home. He ran out of gas in a week's time and needed to rely on truck deliveries of the jerricans that had been stowed on the beach at Normandy. The First Army, which was using twice as much fuel, had the same problem.

After the Americans liberated Paris, the original plan took another twist when it was decided to keep right on going. The supply problem was almost completely ignored, and General Omar Bradley decided: "The armies will go as far as practicable, and wait until the supply system in the rear will permit further advance." But it didn't quite work out that way. As forward divisions moved out, they never looked back. Consequently, they spread themselves out over a wider front than had ever been established in any previous war. That may have been a good thing in terms of tactics, but it was a logistical nightmare as the armies outran their supply lines, their vehicles ran out of gas, and their fighting men went hungry. Most of the supplies they needed were still back on the beach at Normandy, more than three hundred miles away. The French railroads had largely been destroyed, and it was obvious that trucks were the only answer.

The plan that developed into the Red Ball Express was top-secret, just as the invasion itself had been. The secrecy wasn't as much centered around what was going to happen as it was about how such a thing could be accomplished in time to do any good. It involved building a one-way loop road between the coast and Paris and setting up depots at each end, and checkpoints along the way, not to mention training MPs to make sure everything ran smoothly.

Four days after the Red Ball started rolling, some 132 black quartermaster companies, manning more than 6,000 vehicles, were making the round-trip run, and the route had been extended to the front lines, which were more than four hundred miles away by then. The trip took fifty-four hours.

Because it was an around-the-clock all-weather operation, the men had to follow strict rules. All of the vehicles moved in convoys, maintaining a distance of sixty yards between each truck. They kept to a speed limit of twenty-five miles an hour, and at precisely ten minutes before each hour, they all stopped for a ten-minute break. If they were lucky, their break might have been at one of a string of bivouac areas strung out along the route, but mostly they stayed behind the wheel, sometimes eating C rations that they heated on their truck's manifold. The drivers were forced to slow down at night because they couldn't turn on their headlights, which might have attracted enemy bombers. Still, many of the convoys were hit by the pilotless German rockets called buzz bombs, and sometimes the drivers got involved in skirmishes with the enemy along the roadside. All of the men carried rifles in their cabs, and a few of the trucks were equipped with anti-aircraft guns. If a truck was hit by enemy fire or had a mechanical breakdown, it was pulled off to the side of the road, where roving teams of mechanics repaired it on the spot.

By mid–September 1945, about three weeks after the program began, the Red Ball Express was delivering one million gallons of gasoline a day up to the front lines, and the First and Third Armies were able to start rolling again. All of the gas was carried up to the front in five-gallon jerricans, which didn't need any special equipment for handling or for storage. This tactic also had the advantage of making each of the 2.5-ton trucks appear to be identical. There were no tanker trucks to attract enemy planes.

The program was extended beyond its original time frame to allow other units, also mostly manned by black soldiers, to rebuild the railroads and to lay oil pipelines that would make the truck convoys and their jerricans obsolete. By the time the Red Ball drivers stopped making their runs in November, the front lines had gotten still farther away, and the supply trucks themselves were already burning 300,000 gallons of gas a day on their own. Before the operation was shut down, the Red Ball had moved 500,000 tons of supplies to where they were needed, allowing the fighting men to do their jobs. When it went into action, 210,209 African-Americans were serving in Europe, 93,292 of whom became involved in one way or another with the Red Ball Express.

* * *

Not long after the fighting ended, the War Department set up a committee headed by Lieutenant General Alvan C. Gillem to study the question of the use of black troops in the future. The investigation's tone was set by Major General Edward Almond, who had commanded the black 92nd Division, and was one of the first to testify. After asserting, "Negroes are afraid at night," the general reported, " . . . initiative and determination are low by white standards, so is responsibility," and that " . . . they do much good work when not in immediate danger, but freeze up under fire."

The general consensus among the sixty witnesses who appeared before the committee was that "black troops don't run, they just melt away," On the positive side, Frederic Davison, a black officer who had served with 92nd, took the opportunity to offer a rebuttal to General Mark Clark's assertion that the division was "the worst," by testifying that, "The 92nd did not disintegrate as did so many of the Divisions in the Bulge [two full all-white regiments had surrendered during the fighting]. I know that in the 366th, units that were surrounded were wiped out. General Clark . . . misrepresented the facts."

For the most part, though, the committee concluded the army's segregation policies didn't need to be changed, but it offered a better reason than post–World War I investigations had offered. Back in the 1920s, the military had closed the door on integrating its battle units with "scientific" evidence that blacks were incapable of learning the proper skills. Two decades later, the Gillem Committee reported the problem was that, "Leadership qualities had not been developed among the Negro, due principally to environment and lack of opportunity. These factors had also affected his development in the various skills and crafts." While its final report called for more efforts to recruit and retain blacks, it also endorsed continuing existing segregation policies. As others had said before, the Gillem Committee noted: "The Army is not an instrument of social reform." As for the lack of opportunity it had noted, it was made quite clear that there would not be any opportunities available in the future, either. Not in this man's army.

There was change coming in the future, but it would come as a complete surprise to everyone involved. Meanwhile, the GIs who came home from the Second World War had less hope that their lives were going to different than the doughboys who came back from the first war. They had found more opportunities to attract battlefield attention than the men who fought in completely segregated units in 1918, but the military bent over backward to make sure that no one noticed. Suddenly, now that the war was over, black soldiers found themselves right in the spotlight.

Because they had largely been denied combat duty, far fewer blacks than whites had earned enough points to qualify for discharge, and they provided the bulk of occupation troops in postwar Germany. A Senate committee studying the military government there announced that one of the biggest problems it uncovered was the large number of black troops in the army of occupation. Its conclusion: "There is a question whether Negro troops should have been used at all for occupational service because the race question was bound to be encountered since no Negro population is to be found in Germany." What they were saying between the lines was that they expected these black men were going to become involved with white women. Orders had already been issued forbidding interracial marriage. The justification was that these soldiers were forbidden by the laws of their home states to marry outside their own race. General Benjamin Davis, Sr. said that he was not in favor of GIs marrying foreigners—even of their own race—but he went on record opposing an official ban.

The question went beyond marriage. The American press, which had almost completely ignored the black presence in the military during the war began showering them with attention. When photographs were published showing black soldiers dancing with German women, General Eisenhower was deluged with letters of protest. One said: " . . . I do not know where these Negroes come from, but it is likely that if they ever expect to return to the South they very likely are on their way to be hanged or to be burned alive at public lynchings by the white men of the South." It was a self-fulfilling prophecy. There were many lynchings in the postwar South, and beatings of blacks still in uniform as well. Sometimes, the hurt was more subtle. When Lieutenant Christopher Sturkey, who had won a Silver Star fighting with Patton's army as part of the 761st Tank Battalion, arrived home in Detroit, he stopped at a hamburger stand, in full uniform, with campaign ribbons, medal and all, but was turned away by a waitress who informed him, "We don't serve niggers in here."

The fact was that every returning black soldier seemed to face the same prospect. There weren't any homecoming parades like the one for the men of the 369th after the last war, and few expressions of any kind of gratitude. These men were still barred from lunch counters and front seats on public transportation and there were fierce debates raging in every state legislature in the South over whether "those people" should be given the right to vote.

If those men, like the ones who had marched into battle twenty-seven years earlier, had changed anything at all, most of their fellow Americans didn't seem to notice.

8

A Proud Tradition

The triumphal return of the 369th Regiment to New York in 1919 was the first time in American history that nearly the whole country sat up and took notice of what African-Americans could accomplish on a battlefield. The Hellfighters had been denied the right to fight together under their own American flag, and that, too, was a first in America's military history, although the fact is that many hundreds of Negroes had fought and died for their country long before the American flag existed.

Although none of the early records offer specific names or racial references, there are enough accounts sprinkled through Colonial histories to prove without any doubt that the early seventeenth-century settlers along the East Coast frequently called on blacks to help them keep the Indians from overrunning their settlements.

When these colonists found themselves caught in the middle of the spillover of European wars between the British and French at the beginning of the eighteenth century, slaves and free Negroes were accepted into the colonial militias and they were involved in the fighting during Queen Anne's War that took place between 1702 and 1713. Black militiamen also served in the other wars of the period, a series of conflicts that lead up to and included the French and Indian Wars from 1754 to 1763. The militias technically served as units of the British army against the French and their Indian allies, but they were fighting and dying in defense of what had already become the American way of life. Blacks also integrated the maritime service during the same period, and they continued to serve at sea right on through the Revolutionary War, when they were on deck to take part in the creation of the Continental navy.

The blacks who served in the navy back then were either free men or runaway slaves, but many of those who served in the militias were still in bondage, and they were required to turn their pay over to their masters. Either way, though, pay scales for Negroes on both land and sea were equal to the wages that were being paid to whites for the same service And most of those who served in the colonial militias were frequently encouraged to volunteer by a promise of personal freedom, a far more desirable benefit than any pay check.

In South Carolina, for example, the law guaranteed freedom to any slave who killed or captured an enemy in battle. Many slaves earned their freedom this way, and most of the other colonies made similar offers, sometimes offering manumission to any slave who simply volunteered. The catch was that their masters had to approve, and since slaves represented a large financial investment, that approval was never easy to come by. Still, many did join the fight, largely because many slave owners realized that it was better to donate a bit of property to the cause than it was to be forced into the fighting themselves. In 1748, after troops under the banner of the Royal Governor of South Carolina had successfully defended the colony against the French and Indians during the phase of the conflict known as King George's War, a proclamation was issued specifically thanking the colony's black militiamen, who, he noted, " . . . in times of war, behaved themselves with great faithfulness and courage in repelling the attacks of his Majesty's enemies."

The man who is usually considered to be America's earliest black military hero is Crispus Attucks, who was the first Negro to die for the cause of American independence. Born a slave to an African father and an Indian mother in the Massachusetts colony around 1723, Attucks became an accomplished livestock trader. He was allowed to keep some of the money he made in his dealings, which he tried to use to buy his freedom. His master, William Brown, refused to even consider it, so the twenty-seven-year-old slave kept his money and freed himself by running away.

His former master offered a handsome reward for his return, but young Attucks seemed to have vanished from the face of the earth. The most common theory—although still only a theory— is that he made his way to Nantucket where he signed aboard a whaling ship as a harpoonist, virtually all of whom were blacks. This enterprise would have kept him well out of sight. In any event, no one saw Crispus Attucks from the day he ran away, September 30, 1750, until the night of March 5, 1770, when he appeared on Boston Common.

While he was away, the colonists had been seething with anger under British rule. In Massachusetts, people were especially resentful that they couldn't buy anything that didn't come from England, and then had to pay onerous taxes when they did. King George III, added insult to the injury in 1769 when he sent two regiments of soldiers to Boston to keep an eye on his rebellious subjects, and then ordered the locals to pay for their upkeep.

On a fateful night the following spring, Attucks's quiet dinner at a Dock Square tavern was interrupted by the sound of a fight between local men and soldiers on the nearby Common. He went outside and rounded up a large group of bystanders and led them over to where the fighting was going on. Then he placed himself between the soldiers and the crowd. The redcoats responded to the intrusion by firing their muskets and Attucks fell dead along with four others.

Six of the men who had followed him were wounded. The funeral for the victims of what came to be known as the Boston Massacre drew the largest crowd ever seen in the 150-year history of the colony.

Although Attucks is remembered as the first black man to die for the cause of independence, the Revolutionary War itself didn't begin until more than five years later, when Massachusetts volunteers who called themselves Minutemen headed off the British at Concord Bridge on April 19, 1775. There were several blacks among the defenders who showed up that night in response to Paul Revere's warning, "the British are coming," including Lemuel Haynes, who would go on to join Ethan Allen's Green Mountain Boys and see action in the capture of Fort Ticonderoga two years later. That first night, after the opening shots of the war had been fired, Haynes and the others took the fight to the village green at nearby Lexington, and together they routed the invaders.

A few weeks after the Battle of Lexington and Concord, where the British saw a great many black faces staring at them across the lines, the Massachusetts Committee of Safety, which was orchestrating the rebel activities, decided that while they would allow free blacks to join their ranks, slaves would be forbidden to serve. It was an echo of policies in most of the other colonies, enacted out of fear that arming slaves might lead to rebellions, several of which had already been taken place in the South.

This ruling didn't apply to blacks who were already serving. There was a large representation of them among the Minutemen who met the British in the Battle of Bunker Hill two months after the skirmish at Concord Bridge. They managed to drive the enemy back twice before they ran out of ammunition, which often was nothing more than nails and scrap iron poured down the barrels of their cannons. They lost the battle because of their lack of firepower, and not their lack of bravery. However, none of them had any intention of allowing himself to be taken prisoner.

It looked as if they might have to when the enemy commander, Major John Pitcairn, appeared in front of their lines, imperiously demanding their surrender. The Minutemen were frozen in their tracks. No one dared make a move until a black soldier named Peter Salem stepped forward and killed the officer with a ball from his musket that hit the man squarely in the chest. The rest of the Minutemen scrambled away in the confusion that followed. In the post-mortems of the battle, the American commander, Colonel William Prescott, singled out Salem Poore, one of his black soldiers, for special attention, and his report to the Continental Congress, which was signed by fourteen of his top officers, said: "He behaved like an experienced officer, as well as an excellent soldier . . . we only beg leave to say in the person of this said Negro centers a brave and gallant soldier." The new Continental army didn't have any medals to award at the time, but it is certain that if it did, Salem Poore would easily have claimed one.

While the Battle of Bunker Hill was being fought in Boston, the Continental Congress was meeting in Philadelphia to combine all of the colonial militias into a single Continental army. It named George Washington, a slave-owning Virginia planter, as its commander in chief, and although the general had commanded black troops during the French and Indian Wars, and had seemed to be impressed by their performance, he let it be known that he didn't want any Negroes in his new army. One of the first orders he issued was to deny enlistment to " . . . any deserter from the Ministerial [British] Army, nor any stroller [vernacular for a homosexual], Negro or Vagabond." His ruling allowed blacks already serving to continue doing so, but he also stipulated that they should be discharged when their enlistments expired. All enlistments in the Continental army ended officially on December 31, 1775, and although there was an expectation that at least half or more of them would reenlist, General Washington had made that option impossible for black soldiers, regardless of their patriotism or their previous records in battle. The ruling was extended to bar service by Native Americans as well.

The individual colonies generally agreed to the edict and all of them abided by it. But there was another side to the story. Lord Dunmore, the royal governor of Virginia, offered freedom to slaves who would join what he called the Ethiopian Regiment of the British army to help him put down the revolution in his colony. More than three hundred signed up, and they met Virginia's rebel army in August 1775 in a battle they lost decisively, owing more to an outbreak of smallpox than to the colonists' strength. The regiment faded out of existence after that, and the black survivors were evacuated out of Virginia aboard British troop transport ships.

The affair prompted Virginia patriot Patrick Henry to demand that Thomas Jefferson should add "rousing blacks to destroy us" to the list of crimes by King George III that were to be included in the forthcoming Declaration of Independence. Jefferson had already written in his first draft that England had, "waged cruel war itself against human nature itself, violating its most sacred rights of life and liberty of a distant people who never offended him, carrying them into slavery in another hemisphere," but in light of his neighbors' reaction to the Dunmore affair, Jefferson realized the hypocrisy of such a statement and struck it out.

Meanwhile, the Continental army was suffering from a severe manpower shortage. Worse, they were losing the war, and they were still being forced to ignore the availability of nearly 19 percent of the population of able-bodied men that was represented by previously freed slaves. Some of the colonies had already begun winking at Washington's order and were quietly recruiting black men. In 1776, after the Continental Congress established enlistment quotas for all of them, most realized that black recruits were their only answer to filling them. The official order seemed to justify the strategy by requesting that they find men "by draft, from their militia, *or in any other way.*"

In most of the northern colonies, slave owners were being paid a bounty for donating their chattels to the war effort, and in many cases their slaves were serving as substitutes to allow them to avoid being drafted themselves. By the middle of 1776, there was hardly any unit, with the exception of artillery companies, in Washington's army that didn't include black soldiers. A year later, a British officer wrote in his journal: " . . . no regiment is to be seen in which there are not Negroes in abundance, and among them are able-bodied, strong and brave fellows."

There were also black men serving on the British side during the Revolutionary War. The British actively recruited them, offering freedom and a one-shilling enlistment bonus to any slave who would join their ranks. These recruits proved to be especially valuable as guides in this foreign land, and many saw service as laborers as well. But a large number of them were placed in segregated fighting regiments, too, and those whom the Continentals captured in battle were usually held to be used in prisoner exchanges. In many parts of the South, however, they were offered as an incentive to encourage whites to enlist in return for a bonus of one able-bodied slave for every year of service.

But not everyone agreed that this was in the proper spirit of a war that was being hailed as a fight for liberty. Future President James Madison was among them, and he asked the Virginia House of Burgesses, "Would it not be as well to liberate and make soldiers at once of the Negroes themselves, as to make them instruments for enlisting white soldiers? It would certainly be more consonant with the principles of liberty, which ought never to be lost sight of in a contest for liberty."

The lawmakers were unmoved.

The southern colonies were especially hard-pressed for manpower to help fight this war for liberty, not only because the enemy was luring their slaves away, but because a large percentage of the white population were Tories who weren't at all interested in fighting for their own freedom from the mother country.

Officials from Georgia and South Carolina put their heads together and came up with a scheme that they expected would raise 3,000 black troops to help fight the war under white officers. They offered slave owners one thousand dollars for every black man donated to the cause, and the slaves themselves were promised their freedom and a fifty-dollar bonus at the end of their service, although they wouldn't be paid anything at all until then.

But the idea was stillborn. The South Carolina legislature noted that it was " . . . received with horror by the planters, who figured to themselves terrible consequences." Even though British troops were already marching in the direction of Charleston, the lawmakers apparently considered the consequences of war in the streets less preferable than taking slaves away from the local planters, and they voted down the proposal unanimously. The Georgia legislature followed their lead.

By the time the British finally surrendered in 1781, there were thousands of black veterans to deal with. Nearly all of them had been promised their freedom in return for fighting, but there were also many black veterans among them who had simply run away from their masters, who wanted them back. In the controversy that followed, it was generally decided to forget the promises and return all of the former slaves to bondage regardless of how they might have made their way off the plantations.

Many of them were rescued by the departing British, and thousands of blacks were loaded aboard their ships that carried them to the Caribbean or to Canada. Not all of them found freedom at the end of their voyages; but courtesy of the defeated enemy, an estimated 20,000 former slaves left the country after the end of the war that had been fought to secure "liberty and justice for all."

America's next war had its roots in a British attack on the American naval vessel *Chesapeake* near Norfolk, Virginia, in June 1807. The Royal Navy was looking for deserters among her crew, but the majority of them turned out to be black Americans. It shouldn't have come as a complete surprise, considering the fact that about one-sixth of the U.S. Navy's personnel at the time were black sailors. The British were also guilty of what was known as "impressment," the kidnapping of sailors to man their ships, for more than 25 years. This was the last straw.

The incident was one of thousands of such forced boardings of American ships that took place in the early years of the nineteenth century, but as far as American public opinion was concerned, it was one too many. It led to a boycott of English imports, along with strong calls for going to war against Britain once again. The calls were answered by President James Madison who secured a declaration of war from Congress on June 18, 1812. It seemed foolhardy. The British navy had a thousand warships, and it had defeated Napoleon's mighty French navy during the Battle of Trafalgar less than five years earlier. The American navy consisted of only seventeen ships at the time, and not one of them was a battleship.

The fleet grew by ten vessels in the early days of the war when Oliver Hazard Perry took on the job of removing the British from Lake Erie and eliminating their hold on what was known as the Northwest Territories extending along the shores of the lake from Ohio into Michigan. New ships needed new crews, and when his superior, Commodore Isaac Chauncey, assigned the men, about 12 percent of them turned out to be black, Perry complained, "The men . . . were a motley set, blacks, soldiers and boys. I cannot think that you saw them after they were selected."

Chauncey fired back a reply: "I regret you were not pleased with the men sent you, for to my knowledge a part of them are not surpassed by any seamen in the fleet, and I have yet to learn that the color of a man's skin or the cut and trimming of the coat can affect a man's qualifications or usefulness. I have nearly fifty blacks on this boat and many of them are among the best of my men."

After his fleet eliminated the British from Lake Erie and drove the enemy north into Canada, Perry became a firm believer in the value of having blacks in his crews. "They seem to be absolutely insensible to danger," he said.

In spite of the enthusiasm of the navy's leaders, the U.S. Army was forbidden to accept even free blacks until 1814, when the war was nearly over. After he learned that the enemy was building up an invasion force (including more than a thousand Negro troops) on the island of Jamaica to launch an attack on New Orleans, the American commander on the Gulf Coast, General Andrew Jackson, knew that was going to need to beef up his army, and he accomplished it by calling on the area's community of free blacks, which was by far the largest anywhere in the country, in this proclamation:

Through a mistaken policy, you have heretofore been deprived of a participation in he glorious struggle for national rights in which our country is engaged. This no longer shall exist.

As sons of freedom, you are now called upon to defend our most inestimable blessing. As Americans, your country looks with confidence to her adopted children for a valorous support, as a faithful return or the advantages enjoyed under her mild and equitable government. As fathers, husbands and brothers, you are summoned to rally around the standard of the Eagle to defend all which is dear in existence . . .

The appeal went on to promise every volunteer a cash payment of $124 and a land grant of sixty acres. Jackson also promised them that they would serve under black noncommissioned officers whom they could choose for themselves, but that the higher officers would, of course, be white. He concluded his appeal by telling the prospective black recruits that they would be serving in segregated units. But that, he said, was to their advantage:

"Due regard will be paid to the feelings of freemen and soldiers. You will not, by being associated with white men in the same corps, be exposed to improper comparisons or unjust sarcasm. As a distinct, independent battalion or regiment, pursuing the path of glory, you will, undivided, receive the applause and gratitude of your countrymen."

Reading those words today, one might be prompted to say, "How quaint." But it would remain the standard justification for the army's segregationist policies for the next 134 years.

In spite of Jackson's transparent jingoism, more than four hundred free blacks accepted his offer, along with another hundred or so slaves who were put to work building defenses in anticipation of the British invasion of New Orleans. The free blacks were assigned to two segregated battalions, but even then, they were not "undivided." One of the units was reserved for men who had been part of the local community, and the other for recent refugees from the island of Santo Domingo.

After the British arrived, the two black battalions were teamed up with a strange mix of fighting men that included roughshod Mississippi River riflemen, Jean Lafitte's pirate crews, and a handful of Choctaw Indians. Together they faced an experienced British force that outnumbered them by more than two to one, but in two hours of fighting, they evened the odds by wounding 1,400 of the enemy and killing 700, including their general, Edward Packenham, while suffering only negligible losses. It was the last time any foreign country entertained any idea of invading the North American continent. Jackson wrote later: " . . . I have always believed he [General Packenham] fell from the bullet of a free man of color, who was a famous rifle shot."

After the battle, which was actually won after the peace treaty had been signed half a world away, Jackson and his men were honored with a celebration and parade through the streets of New Orleans, during which the black volunteers drew the loudest cheers. The parade was repeated every year after that, but the colored veterans were never allowed to march again. The men were mustered out of the army the day after the battle, and Washington officials issued a formal statement that, New Orleans notwithstanding, "A Negro is deemed unfit to associate with the American soldier." All of the state militias seconded the idea, except for Louisiana's; and, to all intents and purposes, despite General Jackson's appeal that had called it a "mistaken policy," there were no black men serving their country, except for the ones who were still filling out their enlistments.

And their days were clearly numbered.

In the years before the Florida Territory was acquired by the U.S. in 1818, it had been a favorite haven for generations of runaway slaves. In 1835, General Jackson led an army there to recapture them. It gave the Americans another taste of the kind of fighters Negroes could be. Along with the Seminole Indians, the former slaves held off the U.S. Army for seven long years, after which one general noted: "Throughout my operations I found the Negroes the most active and determined warriors; and during the conference with the Indian chiefs I ascertained that they exercised an almost controlling influence over them."

Another officer reported, "The Negroes would stand and fight back, even with their bare hands."

Despite that evidence, when the United States went to war with Mexico eleven years later, the rule against using black soldiers in combat was strictly enforced with no exceptions. It would be the only war in the country's history that didn't depend on African-American fighting men.

If there was a reason behind the segregationist policies of the American military, which wasn't part of the pattern in many of the individual states, it was a fear among Southern slave owners that armed blacks might one day rise up against them. Southern members of Congress dominated national affairs in the early years of the republic because it was in their own best interest to exert their influence, and because together they represented the majority of the population. Ironically, that majority came from the presence of the slaves they owned. Even though they themselves didn't regard them as citizens worthy of the same rights as everyone else, they did count in the population figures that determined congressional representation. In 1790, when the country's first census was taken, nearly 700,000 slaves were reported to be part of the American population. Fewer than 41,000 of them were living north of the Chesapeake Bay.

Things began to change in the new century. By 1850, thanks to waves of foreign immigration, the North had outstripped the South both in terms of population and economic growth, and that tipped the balance of political power. Representatives of both sections had been disagreeing with one another since before the Constitution was adopted, but now their differences of opinion were beginning to seem impossible to resolve. The Northerners pushed for a strong national influence in the country's affairs, and the Southerners dug in their heels in favor of regional power, which they called "states' rights." The majority rules in a democracy, and, as blacks knew very well, the minority must submit to its will. In this case, the

Southerners found themselves in a minority position in the shaping of national policy, an unfamiliar role they didn't like at all.

About the only compromise that seemed to work was to simply ignore the problem, and the new country settled into the concept of two separate societies. Southern planters, who needed slaves to keep their operations viable, began to justify slavery as an institution that took care of an otherwise helpless race. Northerners picked the argument apart and generally painted a picture of the typical white American in the South as shiftless, lazy, and overbearing. That drew a counter caricature among Southerners, who characterized Northern industrialists as greedy money-grubbers and the people who worked for them as dullards. Over time, the stereotypes on both sides led to hate, and the hate led to war.

As new states began coming into the Union in the early nineteenth century, an increasing number of them chose to join as "free" states, with clauses in their constitutions forbidding slavery. The Southerners regarded that as a sign that there would soon be an antislavery majority in the federal government, and it would have the power to sweep the institution out of the country altogether.

The signs couldn't have come at a worse time. As the eighteenth century came to an end, markets for southern produce were drying up, and the institution of slavery seemed to be fading into history. But then a new machine called the cotton gin made it simpler to process raw cotton. As prices dropped, demand mushroomed. It meant that more land was planted in cotton, and that increased the need for slaves. Witnn less than fifty years after the machine was introduced in 1793, the southern slave population more than quintupled from 700,000 to 4 million, and the price of an individual slave went up from $200 to $2,000. Southern planters now had a huge investment to protect.

The inevitable crisis that seemed to be coming with the admission of more "free" states was averted several times through congressional compromises, but it came to a head when Abraham Lincoln was elected president in 1860 by virtue of electoral votes from the Northern states. (His plurality amounted to only 40 percent of the popular vote, as Stephen Douglas garnered 29 percent in the divided field of four candidates.) Even though he had promised that his new Republican party wouldn't interfere with the status quo on the issue of slavery, within three months of his election—even before his inauguration—eleven Southern states seceded from the Union and formed the Confederate States of America.

Although black Americans had a personal stake in the outcome of the Civil War, there wasn't any rush to recruit them to fight on either side. But blacks themselves let it be known that they were ready, willing, and able to serve. A group of African-Americans from Boston sent a petition to Washington: " . . . We are ready to stand by and defend our government as the equals of its white defenders—to do so with our lives, our fortunes, and our sacred honor, for the sake of freedom and as good citizens; and we ask you to modify your laws, that we may enlist."

The petition pledged to raise an army of fifty thousand men, half of whom would be natives of the South and could provide an invaluable service though their knowledge of the countryside and the nature of the enemy. It also promised the services of black women eager to serve as nurses, seamstresses, and "warriors if need be," but officials in Washington weren't interested. Neither was the white population, most of whom were blunt about their conviction that this was a "white man's war."

President Lincoln himself repeatedly expressed his opposition to allowing African-Americans to bear arms. He couldn't have been swayed by any arguments that the Negro race had a stake in the war because he didn't consider it a fight to end slavery at all. "My paramount object in this struggle is to save the Union," he wrote. "If I could save the Union without freeing any slave, I would do it, and if I could save the Union by freeing all the slaves I would do it; and if I could save it by freeing some and leaving others alone, I would also do that. What I do about slavery and the colored race, I do because I believe it helps save the Union; and what I forbear, I forbear because I do not believe it would help save the Union."

Naturally, the Confederate states had no intention of allowing African-Americans to put their lives on the line for the right to live in bondage. Jefferson Davis, the president of the Confederacy, said, "I do not want independence if it is to be won by the help of the Negro. The justification of slavery in the South is the inferiority of the Negro. If we make him a soldier, we concede the whole question." But since blacks represented their major labor pool, it was only natural that the Confederacy recruited slaves by the thousands to help the cause by building fortifications, bridges, and roads, and working in the factories that were turning out the weapons of war. Many were also dragooned into hauling supplies up to the front lines, and some men of color were already there in the role of servants to their masters who had volunteered for the officer corps. It may have considered the Negro to be "inferior," but the Confederate army wasn't above asking for his help.

One of the initial reasons why African-Americans were turned away from Union army recruiting stations after war broke out was that everybody in official Washington, from President Lincoln on down, was certain that it wasn't going to last long enough to risk losing the support of slaveholders in border states that supported the Union. In fact, the first call for recruits was limited to 75,000 volunteers and their standard enlistment was for just ninety days.

Their expectation of a short war started to fall apart during the summer of 1861, when Confederate troops ripped through the Union forces during the first Battle of Bull Run in Virginia. It prompted former slave, Frederick Douglass, who was serving as an adviser to the president, to say, "Colored men were good enough to fight under Washington, but they are not good enough to fight under McClellan [the Union army commander]. . . . The side which first summons the Negro to its aid will conquer."

In spite of Douglass's advice and that expressed in newspaper editorials calling for black participation, when Lincoln issued a call for 300,000 volunteers in July 1862, he again refused to lift the color line. But not long afterward, when Congress softened the rules to allow state militias to begin recruiting blacks to serve in support units, the president signed the bill into law. But he made it clear that he didn't expect it to open the door and allow Negroes to serve in combat. He backed up his point of view when his Secretary of War, Simon Cameron, announced that he intended to allow blacks to be armed. He was given a new job as ambassador to Russia, far from the conflict.

Lincoln's own views changed before he issued his Emancipation Proclamation on January 1, 1863. The proclamation didn't actually free very many slaves because it limited emancipation to persons held in slavery "within any state . . . in rebellion against the United States." Since none of those states recognized Lincoln's authority, it was a moot point. But because the proclamation declared that these former slaves would be "forever free," from that moment on, even if the rebels came back into the fold, it also made it possible for Union troops to liberate slaves as they marched through the South. And because the proclamation authorized these free blacks to be "received into the armed forces of the United States," it was a signal that Negroes would at last be welcomed into the Union army. It had been nearly twenty months since the first shots of the war had been fired on Fort Sumter, South Carolina, on April 12, 1861.

Even without Lincoln's blessing, it had clearly been only a matter of time before black soldiers were going to be allowed to shoulder rifles. Long before Congress began debating the fine-tuning of the law in order to allow blacks to be recruited into service units, Union General David C. Hunter managed to get around the rules by paying recruits out of his own pocket when he put together a company of runaway slaves for the garrison on Saint Simons Island off the Georgia coast. His successor, General Rufus Saxon, secured permission to expand it, at government expense, into a five-thousand-man regiment, and it evolved into a unit called the First South Carolina Colored Volunteers. The regiment's existence was recognized officially at the end of January 1863, a few weeks after the Emancipation Proclamation made it legal. But by then some other black units were already in the fight.

During the summer of 1862, James H. Lane, an officer in the Kansas militia, disobeyed War Department orders and called for volunteers to create an all-black regiment to help him deal with the brutal Confederate raider William Quantrill. Five hundred black men responded to his call, and the First Kansas Colored Volunteers became a unit of the Union army on January 13, 1863, about two weeks ahead of the South Carolina regiment.

The Kansas and South Carolina outfits were the only ones raised during the war that were made up entirely of men who had come directly from slavery, but the Confederacy regarded all black Union soldiers as "slaves in rebellion." Any of them who were captured, regardless of their prewar status, were considered runaways rather than prisoners of war. In many Southern states, the punishment was execution.

The first black troops who actually served in the Union army were three regiments of the Louisiana Native Guards which were mustered-in one at a time between September and November 1862.

After Louisiana seceded from the Union, its governor assigned a regiment of free blacks to defend the city of New Orleans. When

Union Admiral David Farragut took the city in April 1862, the regiment surrendered, but it refused to evacuate along with the retreating rebel troops. Their job was to defend New Orleans, they said, and now they would just stay where they were and defend it against the Confederates. General Benjamin Butler, who had led the land attack, was faced with the job of occupying the city anyway, and he was more than happy to accept their offer of help. He was so pleased with the idea, in fact, that he issued a call for other free blacks in the area to become part of his army of occupation. More than a thousand men joined up within less than two weeks, and with that, the three regiments of the Louisiana Native Guards, brought together as the Corps d'Afrique, switched sides and joined the Army of the United States, whether it was legal to do so, or not.

Although black enlistment was declared acceptable, and even encouraged, after the first day of 1863, there was no stampede among African-Americans to sign up.

Like their neighbors in the other New England states, officials in Massachusetts were grateful for the opportunity to help fill the enlistment quotas that the War Department had saddled them with, and they didn't waste any time establishing the 54th Colored Regiment. But after six weeks of scouring the state for volunteers, their new regiment still had less than a hundred men.

Among the people they called on to help turn things around was Frederick Douglass, who had already gone on record in favor of black participation when he told his fellow African-Americans that, "a war undertaken and brazenly carried on for the perpetual enslavement of colored men calls logically and loudly for colored men to help suppress it." Specifically addressing the situation in New England, he said, "Massachusetts now welcomes you to arms as soldiers. She has but a small colored population from which to recruit. [There were about 5,000 free blacks living in the Bay State at the time.] She has full leave of the general government to send one regiment to the war and she has undertaken to do it. Go quickly and help fill up the first colored regiment from the North." His oratory did the trick, and the 54th was up to speed and ready to fight by June 1863. Among the men who marched off to war in the regiment were two of Douglass's own sons.

As Douglass had pointed out, because the pool of potential black recruits was limited in Massachusetts, recruiting agents were sent into other states and even to Canada to find men who would be willing to serve, and in the end, there were almost as many men from Pennsylvania as from Massachusetts in the 54th Regiment. Meanwhile, recruiters from Pennsylvania as well as other states had also been out beating the bushes well beyond their home bases. Many of them went into the Deep South to find former slaves in Union-held territory, but they quickly found out that the federal government had beaten them to it. As soon as it had permission to recruit African-Americans, the War Department set up the Bureau of Colored Troops and charged it with the responsibility of gathering former slaves into fighting units.

The War Department still depended a great deal on the quotas it set for the individual states, though, and all eyes were on the 54th Massachusetts Infantry when Bostonians turned out in force to give them a grand send-off the day they they boarded a ship that would carry them off to the war. The regiment first saw action at James Island, off Hilton Head, South Carolina, on June 3, 1863, and it became famous a month later in a heartbreaking unsuccessful attack on rebel forces at nearby Fort Wagner. Their charge on the rebel fortress, during which Sergeant William H. Carney became the first Negro winner of the Medal of Honor, made the 54th the most famous black regiment in the fight, and it brought new life to the efforts to recruit African-American soldiers throughout the North. Men of the regiment were also credited with saving the Union army during the first disastrous Florida campaign the following winter. More than a century later, its record became well known to us through the 1989 film, *Glory*, which was centered on the story of the Fort Wagner attack.

Every time the men of the 54th charged into battle, they shouted, "Three cheers for Massachusetts and seven dollars a month!" These men were fighting the enemy, but they were also fighting the government for the right to earn the same pay as white soldiers. The difference was seven dollars a month. Blacks were technically paid ten dollars a month, compared to fourteen for whites, but they had three dollars deducted every month to cover the cost of their uniforms. John Andrew, the governor of Massachusetts, went to Washington to have the situation corrected, but he was told: "The duty of the colored man to defend his country . . . is the same as that with the white man. It does not depend on, nor is it affected by, what the country pays. The true way to secure her rewards and win her confidence is not to stipulate for them, but to deserve them."

Governor Andrew, whose state had two black regiments in the fight by then, the 54th and 55th, persuaded his legislature to split the difference and pay the men the seven dollars a month that they had already proven they deserved beyond any doubt. But the men of the 54th rejected the offer. They said that they had enlisted as equals, and they'd rather get no pay at all than accept less from Washington. They even put their money where their mouths were, and they refused to accept their federal paychecks for three straight months.

Other black regiments protested in their own way. Some staged sit-down strikes; others threatened to desert. One black infantryman wrote to President Lincoln: " . . . we have done a soldier's duty. Why can't we have a soldier's pay?" But nothing was done until a year later, in mid–1864, when Congress got around to passing a bill equalizing all military pay, as well as all allowances for such things as food, clothing, and housing, with no regard to race or duties performed.

The heroism of the 54th Massachusetts and other black regiments went a long way to changing public opinion about African-Americans as fighting men. During the summer of 1863, rioters in New York City protesting against the military draft had concentrated on hunting down and killing the city's blacks, partly because they had been exempted from conscription. But when black volunteers marched off to war from there before the year ended, the *New York Times* noted in an editorial:

> Eight months ago, the African race in this city were literally hunted down like wild beasts. They were shot down in cold blood, or stoned to death, or hung to trees or to lampposts. . . . How astonishingly all this has changed! The same men who could not have shown themselves in the most obscure street in the city without peril of instant death . . . now march in solid platoons, with shouldered muskets, slung knapsacks, and buckled cartridge boxes down through the gravest avenues and busiest thoroughfares to the pealing strains of martial music, and everywhere are saluted with waving handkerchiefs, with descending flowers, and with the acclamations and plaudits of countless beholders.

But "acclamations and plaudits" were not universal in the cities of the Northeast. Not far away in Philadelphia, there had been a strong, although less violent, opposition to allowing African-Americans to get into the war, and a local newspaper, calling the idea "a dangerous experiment," told its readers that it was a "gross outrage" against the country's white freemen to ask them to serve in the same army as blacks. Despite the city's having the largest Negro population of any in the North, and that the local chapter of the Union League had issued a call for the formation of a colored regiment, there was virtually no public support for the proposal in the City of Brotherly Love. Pennsylvania's governor, Andrew Curtin, who would ultimately have to approve the formation of such a regiment, had already signaled where he stood on the issue with an order that prohibited the black regiments from other states from passing through the Keystone State on their way to the war.

Then the war came to him.

After Confederate cavalry dashed over the Mason-Dixon Line into Pennsylvania and captured the town of Chambersburg on June 15, 1863, Governor Curtin issued a desperate call for volunteers to help defend the state capital at nearby Harrisburg. Although his position on race was well known, he neglected to draw any distinctions on who was or wasn't qualified to do the job, and Philadelphia's black churches began ringing their bells wildly to draw their faithful to answer the call.

About one hundred black students responded, and marched off in the direction of Harrisburg a few days later under the flag of the Philadelphia militia. But when they got there, they were informed that they weren't the kind of volunteers that had been requested. The local military commander explained that it had nothing to do with their color, but that, according to the letter of the law, black men could serve only after enlisting for three years, and the War Department hadn't yet authorized the State of Pennsylvania to allow it. As the temporary volunteers were making their way back home, they had to skirt their way around a horde of more than seventy-five-thousand Confederate troops going the other way. Another week would pass before word came from Washington that the black Philadelphians were now welcome to join the U.S. Army. But by then, if they expected to help defend their state's capital, they were going to have to fight their way through the rebel lines to get there.

The resulting regiment, the Sixth Colored Infantry, was trained and ready for combat by early October 1863, when they were sent to Yorktown, Virginia to be joined by three other all-black regiments. Their first major assignment was attacking the city of Petersburg to isolate the Confederate capital at Richmond. They gave such a good account of themselves in the initial assaults that General Grant himself said, "Too much credit cannot be given to the [black] troops for the energy and fortitude displayed during the last five days. Day and night has been all the same, no delays being allowed on any account." Their own commanding officer, General William Smith, went his boss one better when he proudly wrote that, "No nobler effort has been put forth today, and no greater success achieved than that of the Colored Troops."

President Lincoln visited the battlefield not long afterward and requested in advance, "I want to take a look at those boys. I read with greatest delight the account given . . . to the Secretary of War how gallantly they behaved."

After the door was finally pushed open, more than 180,000 black soldiers went into the Civil War in segregated units that were designated the "United States Colored Troops." All of them served under white officers, whom Confederate leaders promised they would hang for treason if they were ever captured. (In fact, several white officers were executed for the "crime.") The African-American troops served in 120 infantry regiments, 7 cavalry regiments, 5 engineer regiments, and 10 artillery companies. One of out of every ten soldiers who served in the Union army during the Civil War was a black man. About 3,000 of them were killed in combat, and another 70,000 died later of battle-related wounds or disease.

Most significantly, 22 of these men who had previously been turned away from recruiting stations earned Medals of Honor during the war. They were among the first that were ever awarded to America's fighting men.

The Confederacy resisted arming blacks until almost the very end of the war, when General Robert E. Lee wrote: "We must decide whether slavery shall be extinguished by our enemies and the slave used against us, or use them ourselves at the risk of the effects which may be produced upon our social institutions. . . . We should employ them without delay." On March 13,1865, President Jefferson Davis signed legislation that would make it possible: the Negro Soldier Law. It called for recruiting 300,000 former slaves into the Confederate army, each of whom would be given his freedom after serving, provided that their owners agreed. A few hundred were actually signed up, but General Lee surrendered three weeks later, and their services were never really utilized.

After the shooting stopped, the Union army was drawn down to sixty-seven regiments including the 24th and 25th all-black infantry and the Ninth and Tenth Colored Cavalry, all four of which were posted west of the Mississippi where they wouldn't offend—or inflame—the defeated South.

Almost as soon as the Tenth Cavalry arived at Fort Leavenworth, Kansas, in 1867, its men were made aware that while slavery was dead, racism was still very much alive. They were assigned quarters in the middle of a swamp, and their commanding officer censured them routinely for having dirty uniforms or muddy boots. He also strictly enforced a rule that no black cavalryman could come within fifteen yards of a white soldier. They were shortchanged in the supplies they were issued as well. On average, their horses were more than twelve years old, and many of the beasts were crippled veterans of the recent war. Their hand-me-down saddles and other tack had seen hard use, too, and were issued, despite badly in need of repair.

But the men of the Tenth Cavalry had other things on their minds. Their mission was to guard the property of the Kansas-Pacific Railroad and to protect the men who were laying its tracks. They got their first taste of action on August 2, 1867, a few days after they arrived. Three hundred Cheyenne Indian braves attacked a troop of two officers and thirty-four soldiers. During six hours of hard fighting, the mounted soldiers decimated the invaders and lost only one of their own men. Sergeant William Christy became the first casualty of this new war on the Great Plains.

The troop, augmented by men of the Kansas militia, tracked down the hostile Cheyenne warriors, but by the time they caught up with them, the Indians' strength had increased to more than a thousand against their number of fewer than one hundred. Despite these odds, they managed to dislodge the enemy. This action earned the black soldiers a reputation for fierceness among the red men, who began calling them the Wild Buffaloes. The name stuck for about a decade until writers and reporters arrived on the scene and wrote about their exploits. They gave the new name of Buffalo Soldiers to all of the black troops on the western frontier.

Not long after the Tenth Cavalry went into action, the federal government attempted to solve the Indian "problem" by relegating 270,000 Native Americans to reservations in hopes of keeping them away from white settlements and railroads. The Cheyenne and Arapahoe were removed to southwestern Oklahoma and Kansas; the Apache went to southern New Mexico and Arizona; and the Sioux, Northern Cheyenne, Crow, and Shoshone were asigned a territory stretching across the Dakotas, Minnesota, and Nebraska, as well as parts of Montana, Wyoming, and Colorado. The job of enforcing the treaties that defined these reservations, and keeping the Indians and white settlers apart, was laid at the feet of the Buffalo Soldiers.

The first of the treaties was broken only weeks after it was signed when white settlers torched an Indian hunting camp on the plains. When the Native Americans retaliated, the army marched against them. The pattern would continue almost without any letup for more than thirty years.

In 1873 parts of the Tenth Cavalry were moved to West Texas, where they joined with the Ninth, and the two black infantry regiments to take over peacekeeping duties in the so-called Great Staked Plain—Apache country extending across New Mexico and east into Texas. Of all of the army's posts, the string of forts near San Antonio were easily the loneliest of all the army posts on the wild frontier. They were collections of jerry-built sod houses and rough wooden structures filled with lice and other vermin, and the men generally preferred to live in tents outside the perimeter or even sleeping under the stars.

The commander of the 25th Regiment reported: "I have visited [their] quarters several times during the past summer to find everything saturated with rain, the floor full four inches deep of mud and the men sitting at meals with their feet in more than an inch of water and their backs being defiled with ooze from the dripping dirt roof."

Their diet consisted mostly of salt pork and bread that they made for themselves from weevil-contaminated flour. Military historian S. L. A. Marshall wrote: "If the troops of the Indian-fighting army craved fresh fruits or vegetables, they had either to grow them or steal them. And they did both."

Their uniforms weren't at all suited to the climate, so most of the men bought buckskin clothes or made them for themselves. They also abandoned their military caps for broad-brimmed hats that gave them more protection from the sun.

But if they were badly fed and clothed, the most pervasive problem that faced these black troops was boredom. The nearest evidence of civilization west of them, which they found out the hard way, was weeks of hard marching away. On one cavalry mission, the troopers covered an average of thirty miles a day for seven months without seeing another human face.

Their overall mission was to sweep the plains of hostile Indians, and they were usually successful at it. They were also given the job of mapping the territory and locating places where crops could be grown and cattle grazed, and they were successful at that, too. But after they opened the plains for white settlement, they acquired a new enemy in the form of their own countrymen, to whom they represented the forces of law and order, which most of these people had traveled west to get away from. To make matters worse, the local sheriffs and federal marshals seemed to be against the Buffalo Soldiers, too. In one instance, a black scout was shot in the back by a Texas sheriff, and no one even questioned the incident. Not long afterward, a white farmer killed three black infantrymen and was acquitted of the crime by a jury of his peers who never bothered to deliberate over the case before handing down their verdict. And so it went. On the other side of the coin, though, many local communities put their prejudices aside, realizing that the soldiers were protecting them from the even more despised and feared Indians, and that they provided trade for local businesses.

The local authorities frequently called on the black soldiers to help them deal with outlaws, cattle rustlers, and others who made keeping the peace a major challenge in the Wild West of the 1870s and 1880s.

Troopers of the Ninth Cavalry, who were stationed at Fort Stanton in the New Mexico Territory, were kept especially busy because they were just a few miles from the town of Lincoln, which may well have been the most lawless spot on the frontier.

The town was under the thumb of local businessmen Lawrence G. Murphy and James J. Dolan, who owned the local general store, and held contracts to provide food for Fort Stanton and for the Mescalero Indian Agency, both of which they routinely cheated. Even though their partner, banker and cattle rancher Thomas B. Catron, was the local U.S. Attorney, "Cattle King of the Pecos" John S. Chisum managed to steal the Mescalero contract out from under them in the late 1870s and financed the opening of a second general store in Lincoln. Naturally, violence broke out among them, and the local U.S. marshal called out troops from the 15th Colored Infantry to help him break up a sherriff's posse that had stormed the Chisum-backed general store, and killed its owner.

Meanwhile, thirty hired guns had been brought in by the Murphy-Dolan interests to get rid of the competition, and in the confrontations that followed, the sheriff and one of his deputies were ambushed and killed. In the endless number of movies based on such sieges, a white cavalryman or a cowboy in a ten-gallon hat would have ridden into town to get rid of the bad guys. But in reality, it was usually the black Buffalo Soldiers who did the job. In the Lincoln County War, which lasted from 1878 to 1881, they patrolled the streets of the county seat for several months until the War Department ruled that federal troops couldn't get involved in "local politics." The white officers at Fort Stanton ignored the ruling, and sent the black troopers in to keep the peace repeatedly for more than another year until their post commander was replaced early in 1879. During that same year, the Tenth Cavalry alone recovered more than one hundred head of stolen cattle, killed four outlaws and arrested seventeen others in a single three-month period.

Many of the Buffalo Soldiers were also forced to endure openly racist white officers. Among the most notorious of them was

Captain Ambrose Hooker, who was assigned to lead the Ninth Cavalry's E Troop in 1869. In his first day on the job, he opined that he regarded blacks as "a treacherous race, utterly devoid of honorable or truthful instincts." Then he warned his new men that he was going to be "anything but agreeable." He turned out to be as good as his word.

Hooker's treatment of his men went beyond words and far beyond the standards of military discipline. On one occasion, when a squad of troopers shot a squirrel while they were on patrol, he reassigned the men to sentry duty and ordered each of them to shoulder a forty-pound log rather than a rifle. After another patrol fired into a flock of turkeys, Hooker demoted their sergeant to private and then ordered him to walk a beat handcuffed with a dead turkey tied to his back, "until it rots."

When the Ninth was sent out into Apache territory, Captain Hooker arbitrarily reduced the night guard over the troop's horses from the standard eight men to five. Then he took away their saddles and carbines, leaving them with only revolvers to defend themselves against the Indians, who were notorious horse thieves, not to mention fierce fighters. The Apache attacked, of course; all five men were killed, and sixty-eight horses vanished into the night. Hooker blamed the victims. "They must have been asleep," he raved. He ordered all five men buried in a common grave and told the soldiers assigned to dig the pit that they should make it extra-large because he threatened that any man who spoke up against him would wind up six feet under as well.

This time, there was an official investigation of Hooker's command. He denied all the testimony of his men, saying that the things he did were intended simply to "impress on them the difference between soldiers and 'cornfield niggers.'" In recognition of his previous good record, Hooker kept his job, and he and his men were assigned to join an expedition to flush out the Apaches. Of the three battalions that rode out, his was the only one that never engaged the enemy, and Hooker faced charges that he had purposely gone to places where he knew he wouldn't have to face any personal danger. His apparent cowardice prompted his commanding officer to start court-martial proceedings against him, but then he thought better of it and let Hooker off with a warning. Fortunately for the men of E Troop, he was also given a leave of absence on grounds of "poor health."

After putting up with such indignities out on the plains for more than fifteen years, the men of the Ninth Cavalry must have thought they'd died and gone to heaven when Major Guy Henry took command of them in 1881.

After leading his men against Mescaleros in New Mexico, Henry began filing reports that were published in the newspaper *Army and Navy Journal*, which had become almost required reading within the military establishment, as well as among the men in the field. The first of them characterized his black troops as "cheerful, willing and obedient," and he went on to say that, in spite of reports that these men were hard on horses, one company under his command ". . . at last muster had but one sore-backed horse, and had marched nine-hundred miles [in one month]." As time went on, Henry's dispatches became even more positive. It was the first time that anyone had anything good to say in print about the Buffalo Soldiers, and the more Major Henry wrote, the harder his men worked to deserve his praise. That pride infected the other black regiments as well.

Henry worked equally hard to turn his troopers into professional soldiers. His intensive marksmanship training program resulted in what he modestly called "the leading garrison in the country" in sharpshooting, and it may well have been. The black soldiers became so highly regarded as fighting men that on at least one occasion would-be Oklahoma settlers, bent on stirring up a war with the Indians so that they could claim off-limits reservation land, backed down without any hesitation when the men of the Ninth Cavalry rode into sight.

In 1890 several troops of the Ninth serving under Major Henry were transferred to the Pine Ridge Agency in South Dakota. A new phenomenon called the Ghost Dance had swept through the Indian nations, and it was at its strongest among the Lakota Sioux, centered in that part of the Badlands. The Native Americans were following the teachings of a Paiute medicine man who predicted that braves who died fighting the white man would return with the power to drive away the invaders, and the now-vanished buffalo would return with them. He also promised them that participants in the dance that prepared them for battle would be protected from the soldiers' bullets by the special shirts they wore.

The Ninth was the first outfit to arrive in the area after this new belief established itself, and their presence unnerved the Sioux. The teachings of the Ghost Dance Society offered them protection against the "white man's bullets," and they weren't sure whether that invincibility extended to guns fired by blacks. They were also all too familiar with the fighting spirit of the Buffalo Soldiers, which was the stuff of legend by then across more than two million square miles of the American West.

Henry's men got their first inkling of the Indians' fear when they arrived at what they had been told was the enemy's strongest outpost and found the native warriors already in retreat even before they rode into sight. Those unfortunate refugees ran into the white Seventh Cavalry, which had earned a dubious place in history fourteen years earlier under General George Armstrong Custer in the battle at Little Big Horn Creek, This time the creek was named Wounded Knee, and the massacre cost the Sioux 153 dead and 44 wounded, well over half of them women and children. When Henry heard of the outrage, he ordered his men back to Pine Ridge to regroup, but his wagon train, which had been bringing up the rear, was cut off from the rest of the column. The horse soldiers swept Sioux braves out of their path as they marched back four miles through a blizzard to save their buddies, and when they finally made it back to Pine Ridge, horses and men alike dropped in their tracks from exhaustion.

But there was still work to be done. The Seventh Cavalry was in trouble again.

When the white troopers found themselves trapped in a canyon on White Clay Creek, they took cover waiting to be rescued, and Major Henry's Buffalo Soldiers were sent out to do the job. After an all-night march, he ordered his men to dismount and divided them into two battalions, which he sent out to scour both sides of the canyon ridge. The Sioux turned and ran when they saw them coming and heard the whizzing bullets from their guns, and the Seventh was saved from the same fate that had nearly ended its existence in the Battle of Little Big Horn.

Though the Negro horse soldiers had been involved in far tougher battles before that one, they had never earned as much acclaim for a victory. Newspapers across the country were wildly enthusiastic in their praise, and one Chicago paper summed it all up:

" . . . Half an hour more and the massacre of 1876 would have been repeated. But at the critical moment, the valiant Buffalo Soldiers of the 9th attacked the Indians in the rear, and turned annihilation into safety."

The Battle of White Clay Creek took place on December 30, 1890, and it was the last of the more than one thousand combat actions in twenty-four separate operations variously called expeditions, campaigns, and wars that began on the heels of the Civil War back in 1865. The fighting didn't end at that point, but the job was essentially finished. The Census Bureau noted in its yearend report that there was no longer a frontier anywhere in the United States. The credit for that belongs largely to the work of the Buffalo Soldiers; black soldiers fighting to subdue Native Americans, who were not free, either.

With the war wound down, all four Colored regiments were kept intact and posted across the West to help keep the peace. The Ninth was kept on at Pine Ridge, but its K Troop was transferred to Washington, D.C., in recognition of the accomplishments of all the Negro troops who had served on the frontier. It marked the first time that black soldiers were posted east of the Mississippi since the close of the Civil War. They stayed there for more than three years, until October 1894, performing ceremonial duties, including escorting President Grover Cleveland in his inaugural parade. The U.S. Army Inspector General noted that they were, "The best instructed cavalry battalion I have yet seen in our army. . . . I have never seen [their] exactness of drill equaled." In spite of such acclaim, the troopers were ordered to rejoin their regiment, which had since been reposted to Fort Robinson, Nebraska, after Washingtonians began complaining that they were getting too much attention in the city.

Their arrival in Nebraska caught the attention of a reporter from the black-owned *Cleveland Gazette*, who informed his readers:

There is a considerable amount of discrimination going on at Fort Robinson. There are three white clerks in the commissary department, two in the post bakery, two in the officers' club and mess room, the post librarian is a white soldier, there are two white soldiers running the post pump house, a white non-commissioned officer is in charge of the post saw mill, and there are five white men in the post quartermaster's department. All of these places are filled by men of the 8th Infantry, of which there are only two companies at the post, in which there are six cavalry companies, all colored.

He might have added that those companies were commanded by white officers. The Buffalo Soldiers, like blacks throughout America's history, had fought well for their country, but the right to become an integral part of their country's army was still eluding them.

The wars in the West, which few Americans considered to be wars at all, secured American claims to all of the territory from the Atlantic to the Pacific; and even before the Great Plains were pacified, the country began looking beyond its new borders for new worlds to conquer.

They found their enemy on the island of Cuba, where a revolution against the Spanish broke out in the early 1890s. U.S. officials claimed to be shocked at the way the colonials were being treated, although they could have found much worse in the treatment of blacks in their own "reconstructed" South. The Spanish, eager to avoid a war, quickly changed their ways, but Congress and influential newspaper barons Joseph Pulitzer and William Randolph Hearst weren't interested in avoiding a war at all. They found their excuse to start one on February 15, 1898, when the battleship *Maine* was blown up in Havana harbor, and the public itself joined in the call for conflict. President William McKinley responded to it, and Congress declared war on Spain on April 19, 1898.

The point of embarkation for troops going into the fight in Cuba was Tampa, Florida, and the first men ordered there was the black 25th Infantry Regiment, shipped down from Montana, where it had recently been involved in labor wars in the mining camps. Their trip across the country was interrupted with wildly enthusiastic demonstrations in every city they passed through, but once they crossed the Mason-Dixon line, the Buffalo Soldiers were brought back to the reality that Jim Crow was still alive and well after all the years they had spent out on the frontier.

The War Department authorized the formation of four new black regiments which, although they served under white officers, were trained by black veterans from the Wild West. There were several black lieutenants in these new outfits, including young Benjamin O. Davis, who would take command of the Harlem Hellfighters exactly forty years later, in 1938. None of them actually saw combat in Cuba, and the only one of them who was authorized to lead troops into battle, Major Charles Young, the third black graduate of West Point, was assigned to teaching duties at Fort Duchesne, Utah. Lieutenant Davis was posted with the Eighth Cavalry at Chickamauga Park, Georgia, where he became a battalion adjutant. The base was the marshalling point for the four new black infantry regiments.

Before war was actually declared, the War Department authorized the formation of ten more all-black regiments because the military believed that Negroes had a natural immunity to tropical diseases like yellow fever, which were virulent in Cuba. Of course, they were wrong. The theory was a close cousin to an age-old belief in the South that black slaves actually thrived working in the hot sun. But the new policy brought more blacks into the ranks, as a percentage of the total, than at any time since the end of the Revolutionary War.

As had happened when the black regiments went west after the Civil War, the quartermasters didn't seem to have given a second thought to the climate. The men being assembled in Tampa were issued woolen winter uniforms, which would become even more uncomfortable after they sailed south to Cuba. When the time arrived to make the move, the ships assigned to carry the Ninth and Tenth Cavalry regiments weren't big enough to accommodate their horses. They had to leave them behind and fight as foot soldiers when they got to the battle zone.

They were the first to go ashore at the village of Daiquiri on June 22, 1898. Although the Spanish defenders had abandoned the place, they lost two men when one of the landing boats capsized. They might have lost more men in the heavy surf, but the First Volunteer Cavalry, commanded by Colonel Theodore Roosevelt, was right behind them and its men made lifesaving duty their first action of the war. The white and black units bonded after that, and they fought side by side during the rest of the short campaign to liberate Cuba.

They met the enemy two days later, and the men of the Tenth Cavalry, on foot, along with Roosevelt's Rough Riders on horseback, destroyed the fortress at Las Guásmas, whose garrison outnumbered them by more than two to one. The heroes of the battle were the black troops, who had honed their skills fighting Indians on the plains. The *Washington Post* reported: "If it had not been for the Negro cavalry, the Rough Riders would have been exterminated."

The next moment of glory for the black troops came two weeks later in the assault on El Caney, on the high ground above the port of Santiago de Cuba. It was an almost impregnable fortress surrounded by open fields, but the men of the all-black 24th and 25th regiments were given the dubious honor of leading the charge against it. One of its men wrote later: "Men were dropping everywhere . . . the bullets were raining in our faces." But the men pressed the attack, depending heavily on the accomplished sharpshooters in their ranks. The soldier's account says: "Thirty or forty of these dead shots were pouring lead into evey rifle pit, door window and porthole in sight . . . the Spaniards were shaken and demoralized . . . our men were shooting them down like dogs . . . the fort was silenced!"

As the battle at El Caney wound down, the 24th Infantry and the Ninth and Tenth Cavalry joined with Colonel Roosevelt's Rough Riders in the most famous battle of the war, the charge up nearby San Juan Hill. They were joined by other white infantry units on July 2, the second day of the assault, and whites and blacks fought side by side as equals, possibly for the last time before the end of World War II, forty-five years later.

The black cavalry units lost some 20 percent of their men at San Juan Hill; but as the *New York Sun* told its readers, "the enthusiasm of the 9th Cavalry was at its highest pitch . . . only annihilation could drive them back; the Spaniards could not."

Lieutenant John J. Pershing, the man who would one day deny the Hellfighters the right to serve in his army during World War I, rode with the men of the Tenth in the battle. In retrospect, he wrote: "We officers of the 10th Cavalry could have taken them into our arms. They had fought their way into our affections, as they have fought their way into the hearts of the American people."

Even Teddy Roosevelt was enthusiastic. "I don't think any Rough Rider will ever forget the tie that binds us to the 9th and 10th Cavalry."

After the war ended following the charge up San Juan Hill, Roosevelt went home to New York to parlay his image as a war hero into a successful campaign to become the state's governor. But his praise of the black soldiers wasn't politically correct, and he started changing his tune. He said that while the men were brave, their success depended entirely on their white officers, and he even "confessed" that he had to force some black deserters back into the fight at gunpoint. No one called him a liar, and he won the election, eventually becoming president of the United States. But there were enough credible eyewitnesses to bravery among the black troops in Cuba that he could easily have been unmasked if anyone cared to do so. The brass in Washington were certainly not inclined to challenge the candidate's charge. The War Department disbanded all the

Negro volunteer regiments in 1899 and demoted all of their black officers to the status of enlisted men.

The War Department had a quick change of heart within weeks, when an insurrection broke out in the Philippine Islands, which had been acquired by the United States after the war, and the American force of twelve thousand was pitted against nearly half a million guerrilla fighters. Two black volunteer regiments were formed hastily, and they joined the veteran Buffalo Soldiers in the islands. After the war was declared over in 1902, the troops were sent back home. But with the Indians, the Spanish and the Filipinos pacified, and almost no threats to democracy remaining, the public had forgotten how much they owed to the black men in their army. Now those men faced hostility and prejudice wherever they were posted.

If anyone believed that the black soldiers had succeeded in their fight to bring equality to the American military, their convictions were swept away on July 28, 1906, when the First Battalion of the 25th Infantry reported to Fort Brown, on the outskirts of Brownsville, Texas. The black troops received anything but a hero's welcome, and the situation got worse with each passing day. They were forbidden to enter most of Brownsville's public buildings, and there was a sign in the public square that said "No Dogs or No Niggers Allowed." After several pushing and shoving incidents, the local rejection came to a head as a rumor swept through the town that a black soldier had tried to rape a white woman, and armed men appeared on the streets randomly firing guns into houses and stores.

Although the garrison was mustered and every man accounted for, the town's mayor claimed to have found army-issue cartridge cases along the road. The resulting inspection of the battalions' rifles showed that none of them had been fired and that every cartridge was accounted for. Nevertheless, a citizens' committee chose to ignore the evidence and declared the soldiers guilty of the shootings, which had resulted in the death of a local bartender and the wounding of a police officer.

Government investigators sent out from Washington reached the same conclusion after two days of hearings, and the troops were moved to Fort Reno, Oklahoma, while the investigation continued. Meanwhile, twelve men had been singled out as the guilty parties, but a Texas grand jury refused to indict them after three weeks of studying the evidence.

Despite this lack of evidence, the army's board of inquiry issued its final report, which concluded that some of the soldiers were guilty of shooting up the town. Since no one seemed willing to give them the proof they needed, the report charged that there was a conspiracy of silence among the troops, and unless the guilty men confessed, the entire battalion would be dishonorably discharged The army's inspector general backed them up, and in November 1906, 167 black soldiers were discharged "without honor," and barred from collecting pensions, back pay, allowance and all other benefits. Twenty-five of the men had served in the army for more than ten years, and one was a twenty-five-year veteran. Six of the men had earned Medals of Honor fighting for their country.

The New Orleans *Picayune* said: "Whatever may be the value of Negro troops in time of war, the fact remains they [black soldiers] are a curse to the country in time of peace."

Although that may have represented a typical Southern point of view, the *New York Times* chimed in that it supported the War Department's decision and that "the soldiers had only themselves to blame."

It all served as a warning that military segregation was as much the wave of the future, as it was a legacy of the past. It would be another forty-two years before it finally came to an end.

9

SEA CHANGE

T IS ESSENTIAL THAT THERE BE MAINTAINED IN THE ARMED
SERVICE OF THE UNITED STATES THE HIGHEST STANDARDS OF
DEMOCRACY, WITH EQUALITY OF TREATMENT AND OPPORTU-
NITY FOR ALL THOSE WHO SERVE IN OUR COUNTRY'S DEFENSE. IT
IS HEREBY DECLARED TO BE THE POLICY OF THE PRESIDENT THAT
THERE SHALL BE EQUALITY OF TREATMENT AND OPPORTUNITY
FOR ALL PERSONS IN THE ARMED FORCES WITHOUT REGARD TO
RACE, COLOR, RELIGION, OR NATIONAL ORIGIN. THIS POLICY
SHALL BE PUT INTO EFFECT AS RAPIDLY AS POSSIBLE, HAVING DUE
REGARD TO EFFECTUATE ANY NECESSARY CHANGES WITHOUT
IMPAIRING EFFICIENCY OR MORALE.

With those words, Executive Order 9981, issued on July 26,
1948, President Harry S Truman officially brought discrimination
to an end in the American military. The military itself was fairly certain that was all it would do, and smugly assumed it could go right
on forming segregated units, but Truman informed them through
a press conference a few days later that his order was intended to end
segregation as well.

As far as the Defense Department (the former War Department)
was concerned, though, they had a way out in the phrase, "as rapidly as possible." Like all government agencies, it was adept at foot-

dragging when the situation called for it, and the brass was convinced that Truman's successor would scrap the executive order after the November election.

It appeared to be a foregone conclusion that there would be a new president by then. Truman had become a laughingstock with in his own party the previous spring when he told them during a speech: "There's going to be Democrat in the White House after 1948, and you're looking at him." When he was actually nominated, much to their surprise, Southern leaders bolted from the party and nominated South Carolina Governor J. Strom Thurmond to lead their States' Rights Democratic party, nicknamed the "Dixiecrats," to what was hoped would be victory. Meanwhile, the Republicans nominated New York, Governor Thomas E. Dewey as their candidate, and made military segregation part of their platform. Nobody was taking any bets that Truman could possibly win the election. But he did, of course, and Executive Order 9981 remained in force.

After all these years, historians still don't agree on why Truman did what he did. The easy answer is that, faced with defeat in the election, he didn't have anything to lose, and possibly the black vote might help turn things around. But Truman's previous record hints that there may be more to it than that. As a U.S. senator from 1934 through 1944, he never failed to support antidiscrimination legislation, and he had been a leader in the fight to establish the Tuskegee Airmen in 1939. During an election campaign the following year, he said, "[I]f any class or race can be permanently set apart from, or pushed down below the rest in political and civil rights, so may any other class or race when it shall incur the displeasure of its more powerful associates, and we may say farewell to the principles on which we count our safety." In another speech during the 1940 campaign, he put it more simply: "In giving Negroes the rights that are theirs, we are only acting in accord with our ideals of a true democracy."

Truman's opinions were strengthened after the end of World War II, when returning black veterans met with the same hostility and resentment that had dogged the doughboys when they came back from France a generation earlier. One event that seemed to sum it all up was the arrest—with no specific charges—of Sergeant Isaac Woodward when he arrived home to Aiken, South Carolina in 1946 after three years of army service overseas. The local sheriff not only beat Woodward, but he struck him so violently on the head with his billy club that the sergeant was permanently blinded. Thanks to intervention by the National Association for the Advancement of Colored People, the sheriff stood trial for his crime. But based on his testimony that Woodward had attacked *him*, the jury found him not guilty, and the whole town turned out to celebrate the "justice" that had been done.

Truman was outraged by the Woodward incident. "As President, I know this is bad," he said. "I shall fight to end evils like this." The first step he took was the creation of the President's Committee on Civil Rights to investigate the new round of racial violence and recommend ways to deal with it. Its final report, issued in late 1947, called for changes in general public policy but it homed in on the military:

> To the citizen in a democracy, freedom is a precious possession. Accordingly, all able-bodied citizens must enjoy the right to serve the nation and the cause of freedom in time of war. . . . By preventing entire groups from making their maximum contribution to the national defense, we weaken our defense to that extent and impose heavier burdens on the remainder of the population.

The military just yawned, and then Congress dozed off after Truman presented it with a civil-rights program based on the committee's report in February 1948. That was when Truman decided to take matters into his own hands. He chose the military for his executive order because it was one the few areas where he had the power to back it up in his role of commander-in-chief of the armed forces.

Change was slow in coming. The barriers against Truman's historic order had existed for more than 175 years. But Truman pushed it along by forming a committee of three white and two black civilians headed by Charles Fahy, a Georgia lawyer. It pushed and prodded the individual services from early 1949 through mid–1950. Its members found out right at the start that while the navy and air force were willing to obey the order, the army and marine corps seemed prepared to put up a fight. The coast guard, which was also covered by the order, although it is an arm of the Treasury rather than the Defense Department, had already begun to integrate on its own.

The navy had enforced some token integration during the war, and wasn't interested in going any further. As a matter of fact, it was quite proud of what it had already accomplished, and was holding itself up as model of leadership in military race relations. The Fahy Committee toured the navy's bases in 1949, and its members were satisfied that blacks, who had once been relegated to kitchen and mess steward duties, were to be found in nearly all specialties, and that there didn't seem to be any evidence of discrimination in training or living conditions. The inspection tour appeared to confirm that the Navy's policy on race was all that it was claimed to be.

Yet the committee members were struck that they had never encountered a black officer, and not too many black sailors, either, for that matter. The fact was that there were only five black officers in the entire navy, and only 5 percent of all its personnel were black. The committee concluded that this was because the navy wasn't making any efforts toward minority recruitment. As one of its members noted, ". . . the Navy knows the general impression among

Negroes is that they can only serve in the messman's branch. [We] take it that silence is exclusion in itself."

The navy countered the charge by pointing out that it didn't have any written policy confining blacks to service as stewards, but that it was just "a tradition." Through other testimony, it was revealed that, in spite of what the committee had seen on its tour, black recruits were still nearly always assigned to the Stewards Branch and were rarely given other duties. Men who served in those roles were not given the status of petty officer, the first step toward rising through the ranks, and they were given only the bare minimum of training, which also kept them in these dead-end jobs.

The committee also questioned the navy's high standards for recruitment and, in the end, concluded that if it were to be in compliance with the executive order, the navy would need to do several things, beginning with bringing its admission standards in line with the army's career requirements. It also recommended an aggressive recruitment campaign to inform the public as well as potential black sailors about open career opportunities, and suggested that it would also have to upgrade the Stewards Branch, allowing its men to hold higher ranks in the same way they could in the other areas of naval service.

Needless to say, the Department of the navy wasn't at all happy with the committee's report card. But after quite a bit of arm-twisting, it finally agreed to accept the Fahy Committee's proposals—although there was one exception.

It promised to call black reservists into active duty as recruiters, and to start an advertising campaign aimed at blacks, as well as restructuring its ROTC program to give more of its scholarships to black candidates. The navy also said it would give stewards the opportunity to move into other specialties, and promote all chief stewards to petty officers. But it would *not* lower its admission standards under any circumstances. In the opinion of its top officers, that would lower the overall quality of naval personnel and, in the end, it would reduce the navy's effectiveness. As a way of getting the Fahy Committee off their backs, they proposed creating a committee of their own that would conduct an in-depth study of enlistment requirements on a specialty-by-specialty basis.

The study dragged on until 1951, when the reorganized Department of Defense ordered uniform entry qualifications for all of the services. But, in the meantime, although the navy was busy implementing its reform agreement, the plan didn't seem to be working in practice as it had appeared on paper that it would. Black sailors were moved out of the kitchens and mess halls into better jobs. But as late as the mid–1950s, almost 52 percent of the navy's black personnel were still in the Stewards Branch, and no white sailors were serving alongside them.

As a part of the navy, the marine corps was theoretically bound to accept the same orders. The Fahy mandate added a requirement that the Corps should do away with its segregated boot camps, but Marine Commandant General Clifton Cates refused to comply. He said that Executive Order 9981 didn't apply to the marines in the first place, and neither did any agreements that the navy might have entered into. He was also adamant about his belief that the only way to make a marine was by training blacks and whites in separate platoons. He did, however, bring the corps into general compliance with the navy's mandate in 1949, right after it was issued. But although race wasn't a factor in choosing specialties any longer, all-black units weren't disbanded.

The Fahy Committee seemed willing to accept Cates's apparent insubordination, and in its final report, it admitted: "Some Negro Marines are still assigned to separate units . . . the effectuation of Navy policy in the Marine Corps is yet to be completed."

There were only about fifteen hundred black marines serving in 1949. In spite of the Fahy Committee's confidence that navy policy would soon take care of their interests, a marine general had flatly stated that the Corps would never allow itself to be integrated. "I think you'd be making a problem instead of solving one," he predicted. But never is a long time, and the marines would eventually drop its color restrictions.

The air force had been established as an independent service in 1947, and it was already on its way to becoming integrated before the presidential order was issued. By the time the Fahy Committee scheduled a meeting with Air Force Secretary Stuart Symington in early January 1949, he informed them that a plan to completely desegregate his branch of the service had already been submitted to the Defense Department, and it had been approved.

In essence, the air force's plan called for doing away with racial quotas and eliminating making assignments based on race, but it did specify that black representation would not be more than 10 percent in any given unit, and it gave individual commanders the right to decide which blacks would be able to serve under them. The Fahy Committee requested that these two provisions be removed and, after the generals agreed, the new policy was sent out to all of its commanders.

The air force plan also called for eliminating the all-black 332nd Fighter Wing, which had grown out of the Tuskegee enterprise, and integrating its men into all-white units, which would set the pace for other such reassignments throughout the service. The ultimate goal was the elimination of all segregated units, but that part of the plan was left without an actual target date.

Many black airmen were convinced that it was all some kind of plot to ease them out, and that new screening rules would land them in assignments for which they would be overqualified. But the Air Force Chief of Staff, General Hoyt Vandenburg, made sure that no such thing could happen. He made it a point that each one of his officers should completely understand the new rules and he made it clear that they would be held personally accountable for any breaches of them. His deputy, General Idwal Edwards, issued the specific instructions:

"There will be frictions and incidents. However, they will be minimized if commanders give the implementation of this policy their personal attention and exercise positive command control. Unless our young commanders are guided and counseled by the senior commanders in unbiased implementation, we may encounter serious troubles . . . It must have your personal attention and personal control."

Some senior officers who considered the plan to be against their personal beliefs quietly resigned their commissions. Some of the men who served under them were court-martialed for racial offenses that would have been considered normal in the military just a few years earlier, and even the commanding general of the Eighth Air Force was threatened with a similar trial for dragging his feet on integrating housing on his bases. But all things considered, integrating the U.S. Air Force went more smoothly than anyone had believed possible.

There was no question that the air force was serious about implementing its integration program, but at the end of its first year, it was forced to admit that it had made a big mistake back at the start. It had underestimated the quality of its own men. Many commanders were genuinely surprised that the black men under them had valuable skills, and to find out how many of them without apparent skills were able to learn them easily. It led to a reassessment of the integration plan and a decision to speed it up. By the end of 1950, more than 95 percent of the blacks in the Air Force were serving in racially mixed units. Within two more years, all of them were.

Meanwhile, the U.S. Army seemed determined that such a thing would never happen within its ranks. Following the lead of his top generals, including George C. Marshall and Dwight D. Eisenhower, who were foursquare on the side of "separate but equal" treatment of troops under them, Army Chief of Staff Omar N. Bradley went on record saying that he believed segregation wouldn't end in the military until after it was eliminated from American society as a whole. Army Secretary Kenneth Royall said that he was convinced that desegregation would actually be detrimental to national defense because the record of blacks in both world wars had proved beyond a doubt (to him, anyway) that they were better qualified for hard labor than for combat.

The army considered itself a special case, and there may have been some justification for it. Unlike the air force, it had few officers at the top who were interested in changing anything at all and, unlike the navy, it couldn't hide its own record on race. Even after the reduction in force that followed World War II, almost 13 percent of the army's enlisted personnel were black. Its officer corps was overwhelmingly from the South, and the bulk of its enlistees came from the South as well. Its public relations policies were in danger because its relationship to local communities through the National Guard made it more vulnerable to the public's opinion than the other services were. The army also had generations of experience in rationalizing what they perceived as the advantages of a segregated fighting force.

Army brass trotted out all of the old arguments when they testified before the Fahy Committee, and they came close to making their arguments stick. But this was not a committee of bureaucrats like those who had previously investigated the army and its racial policies. One word ran like a refrain through all of the arguments, and it was "efficiency." In deposition after deposition, the bottom line was almost always an echo of Army Secretary Royall's assertion that history proves "in the interest of efficient national defense, certain types of units should be entirely or largely confined to white troops."

The first to question that theory was Edwin Kenworthy, one of the committee members, who noted in a letter to Fahy that possibly the army wasn't using its Negro manpower efficiently, and it seemed probable that segregating the 92nd and 93rd divisions during World War II had negatively affected morale, not to mention efficiency.

The committee subpoenaed the army's own files and called in a black personnel expert to testify at their next hearing, where they made the case that separate could never be equal and that the army's policy of forced segregation couldn't possibly give blacks the same opportunities as whites. They informed the generals that, in their view, this was a glaringly inefficient waste of human resources.

Committee members went on to charge that the army's segregation policies were also depriving black soldiers of specialized training, except for the limited specialties that were available in Negro units. That, they pointed out, was grossly inefficient because although training schools were nominally open to blacks, they were being routinely rejected from them on the grounds that the skills they learned couldn't be used by the army.

During the course of the hearings, the committee began to realize that the army was not just trying to mislead them, but was, in fact, lying to President Truman and the Defense Department. Right after the executive order was issued, the army dusted off the report of its Gillem Board, which had concluded in 1945 that blacks should be allowed to continue to serve, but only in small segregated units that might one day be integrated into large white ones. Although the army had filed and forgotten the report, it informed the Defense Department that it had, in fact, become current policy and, as far as they were concerned, that put them in full compliance with Truman's order. A second report, requested a month later, was even more self-serving, and misleading. Simply put, army brass was accustomed to giving orders—not taking them—and it was willing to go to any extremes to keep it that way.

The Fahy Committee wasn't fooled by any of the arguments, though, and in the spring of 1949, it made three demands on the U.S. Army: (1) that military occupational specialties must be filled without regard to race, and that all assignments should be color-blind, too; (2) that racial quotas in army schools should be eliminated; (3) and that the army's quota system limiting black enlistments to 10 percent of the total should be abolished as well, to be replaced by enlistments based on aptitude test scores.

The army ignored these demands, and stormy negotiations continued far into the fall, when President Truman himself stepped in and put pressure on Louis Johnson, his defense secretary, to support the Fahy Committee.

But the battle was still far from over.

In October an order was issued to the army's field commanders to open all specialties to blacks, but when the personnel divisions heard of it, they countermanded the order on the grounds that it violated army policy. The committee used this, and other incidents like it, to wage a campaign in the press, and as leverage in its meetings with Army Secretary Gordon Gray. The army finally caved in with an official directive, issued in January 1950. Personnel would be assigned to military specialties without consideration of race. The army officially abolished the 10 percent enlistment quota two months later. They were the first steps on the road to complete integration, but the end was still a long way off. As the Fahy Committee noted, " . . . the Army intends to do as little as possible toward implementing the policy which it adopted and published."

The Fahy Committee issued its final report, "Freedom to Serve," on May 22, 1950. A little more than a month later, on June 25, more than 60,000 North Korean troops crossed the 38th parallel in an invasion of the South. Five days after that, President Truman ordered American ground and air forces to strike back. It came as a rude shock to everyone who would become involved. Even in World War II, which officially began with a "surprise attack," the men who served had been psychologically and physically prepared for what lay ahead, but in Korea, a military that after World War II had quickly lapsed into a peacetime mode, found itself pitted against an enemy at its peak in motivation and power.

The first unit sent in was the 24th Infantry Division, the last of the all-black units that had been formed after the Civil War. It had been assigned to peacekeeping duties in Japan after World War II, and the majority of black soldiers who were sent to the Far East were absorbed into it. Most of them had not yet seen combat, and in anticipation of shipping out to Korea, the outfit was reorganized with new white officers and new troops rounded up wherever they could be found. Most of the men were strangers to one another. None of them had received any training, with the possible exception of riot control, since they graduated from basic. In most cases, that was four or five years earlier.

Their first days in combat didn't go well. Their lines were riddled by the enemy, which took the town of Yechon on its way to a goal of driving the Americans back to the sea, and the 24th was ordered to counterattack. The official army history of the engagement says that the enemy retreated without a fight, but the Center of Military History tells a different story that squares with reports from the men who were there: that it was a short, but heavy, battle of mortar and artillery. Either way, the town was retaken, and the men of the 24th had scored the first victory of the war. But news of it was overshadowed by the capture of General William F. Dean not far away on the same day, July 21, 1950.

As far as the 24th Division was concerned, the news from the front lines during the next several months was all bad. Officers in the field began sending back reports that the black soldiers weren't performing up to army standards, and the commander of the white 25th Division, whose men were fighting side by side with Negro troops, informed his superiors that the segregated outfit was "untrust-worthy and incapable of carrying out missions expected of an infantry regiment . . . [and threatened to] jeopardize the United Nations war effort in Korea." It was grist for the mills back at the Pentagon, where opposition to integration was still as strong as ever. Actually, had the generals looked more closely and talked to the fighting men themselves, they'd have known that the all-black units were no worse, nor better, than all of the units that were fighting in the early bat-tles of the Korean War. Virtually all of them had been sent over from occupation duties in Japan, and none of them had been trained for combat duties. And if there were reasons to condemn the men of the 24th, there were just as many reasons to single them out for praise, as was the case among all of the units in the fight.

There were official investigations of charges against the black reg-iments. But their conclusions only proved what the Fahy Com-mittee had been telling the Pentagon all along. Their studies had shown that any charges of poor performance against individual black soldiers was a direct result of racial segregation, and that the only way to solve the problem would be to do away with segregated black units altogether and reassign the men into integrated battal-ions. Resistance to the idea was crumbling at last.

While the investigations were proceeding, field commanders in Korea were already disregarding the Army's general orders and they were beefing up their units with black replacement troops. It had less to do with sudden enlightenment than with intolerable per-sonnel shortages, but the army finally began to become desegregated in spite of itself in late summer 1950, and there would be no turning back. A white officer who integrated his outfit noted later that mixed black and white troops worked quite well together mostly because "at a time like that, misery loves company."

At the same time, the army began desegregating its training camps, beginning with Fort Jackson, South Carolina. The post commander was pleased with the result. "I would see recruits, Negro and white, walking down the street, all buddying together," he said. "[T]he attitude of the southern soldiers was that this was the Army way; they accepted it in the same way they acepted getting booted out of bed at five-thirty in the morning." By the end of 1950, every one of the army's training camps had become fully integrated. It took a war to accomplish it, but the army was finally on a steady course toward implementing Truman's order for integration of its troops. By 1953, when the Korean War ended, more than 90 percent of black soldiers were serving in racially mixed units. The four black regiments that had served on the plains and in the Spanish-American War were disbanded, and the two cavalry outfits were transferred to tank battalions, while the infantrymen were distributed among formerly all-white units. The 24th Infantry was disbanded early in the war. One all-black regiment that remained intact was the 369th Antiaircraft Battalion, the heirs to the Hellfighters Regiment, which saw service in Korea between 1950 and 1952. By the time integration was finally complete, the only black regiments that remained were National Guard outfits whose racial makeup was determined by the nature of the communities they served.

The Korean War also pushed the U.S. Marine Corps off the fence in complying with the Truman order. When the war began, there were only about 1,000 black marines in the 74,279-man corps, and almost half of them were serving as mess stewards. Those who were sent to Korea were more often than not ammunition handlers and supply clerks, but in the face of high casualty losses, most of them were reassigned to combat positions. Their performance in the field, fighting side by side with white marines, impressed the commandant, and he began aggressively recruiting more blacks. By the time the war ended, there were more than 15,000 black marines on the front lines in Korea.

In just two years, the branch of the service that had been stubbornly convinced that integration would never come, had become the most color-blind of them all. Every aspect of marine corps life, from boot camp to combat duty, to the assignment of occupational specialities and housing was handled by the numbers rather than by skin color. The corps' own history of this great leap notes: "Records pertaining to black Marines, aside from strength and deployment statistics, are virtually non-existent. With the end of segregation, black Marines have merged into the mainstream of Marine Corps experience."

The Korean War ended in a stalemate and a rather unsatisfactory armistice, leaving the dividing line between North and South Korea exactly where it had been at the start. Its legacy, though, was a racially neutral American fighting force, a state of affairs that was long overdue. But there were still some diehards who felt that they had been blindsided.

General Douglas MacArthur, who commanded all of the troops in Korea, was completely opposed to desegregating the army, but he apparently wasn't aware that it was taking place right under his nose.

When his chief of staff, Lieutenant General Edward M. Almond, discovered that the Second Division's Ninth Regiment included both black and white soldiers, he issued an order to stop the integration right away and, if possible, to reverse it. At the same time, he ordered that no more black soldiers were to be placed in any white units, and where replacements made it necessary, they must be confined to all-black battalions. The division's commander responded by keeping to the letter of the order, if not its spirit, and assigned black replacements to white service units.

President Truman relieved MacArthur of his command in April 1951, and the general had no sooner gone home to drum up sympathy for the way his commander-in-chief had treated him than his former staff in Tokyo revealed the results of an intensive study that concluded: "Negro soldiers can and do fight well when integrated." MacArthur's replacement, General Matthew Ridgeway had already gone on record supporting battlefield integration, and one of his first acts as the new commander was to submit a plan to the Pentagon designed to completely eliminate segregation from the units serving under him. The Department of the Army authorized his proposal, and extended it to include the entire Far East Command on July 1, 1951.

However, despite the changes in the field, military desegregation was not an idea whose time had yet come among the army brass back in Washington. The chief of staff and the defense secretary had both signed off on the idea, but the vice chief of staff and the director of personnel were vehemently opposed to it, and so were dozens of influential officers serving under them. When the war ended, they were still studying plans to form more new all-black units.

Opposition was still strong among commanders in Europe, too. When they were asked to come up with a plan that would comply with the Truman order, they concentrated on combat units, even though the overwhelming number of troops in their command were actually in the service units of an army of occupation. But after a series of half measures, they finally pulled themselves into line and put together a desegregation plan that went into effect on April 1, 1952. The last all-black unit serving in Europe was dissolved two years later, more than six years after President Truman's order called for desegregation to take effect "as rapidly as possible." But it was the last olive out of the bottle. By December 1954, there were no more official restrictions facing black army personnel in any of the service branches.

Getting there had been far from easy. Truman bypassed Congress, which was hostile to the idea, when he ordered military desegregation. Even though most of the negotiating that took place to make it an accomplished fact was done in relative secrecy—to keep the issue from becoming overly politicized—Capitol Hill wasn't completely in the dark. Opposing legislators introduced several bills they would hoped would stifle Executive Order 9981, but all of them died in committee. The United States Army, which had had a reputation of being among the country's most racist institutions, suddenly became a beacon of enlightenment on the subject of integration. But there was still work to be done beyond the gates of military bases.

The ideas that the military had reluctantly accepted were finally brought to the civilian world in 1954, when the U.S. Supreme Court ruled in the case *Oliver Brown et al.* v. *Board of Education of Topeka, Kansas*: "In the field of education, the doctrine of 'separate but equal' has no place. Separate educational facilities are inherently unequal." Most school districts and many politicians put their own spin on the ruling, and schools went right on following segregation restrictions until a year later when the Court clarified its decison and ordered that school segregation must end "with all deliberate speed." But even then, many states, particularly in the South, still refused to allow black children into all-white schools.

Apart from its call for fast action, the Court hadn't imposed any deadline on the order, and although many southern states amended their own laws to bring themselves into line with it, many others decided to wait and see. Chief among them was Mississippi, where white supremacists rose up in revolt. Not only did they fight to keep the educational system lily-white, but they banned the sale of books they didn't agree with and purged their libraries of them, too. They boycotted newspapers and magazines they suspected of having a pro-integration bias, and, when they could, they censored movies and TV shows. Emboldened by the apparent success of the movement, people in other southern states began jumping on the bandwagon, too.

Their opposition led to rioting on the University of Alabama campus in 1956, when a mob showed up to block the registration of a black woman named Autherine Lucy. In its aftermath, politicians started calling for more such "massive resistance." Florida Governor Leroy Collins anounced that his state was "just as determined as any other southern state to maintain segregation," and nearly all of the others passed new laws that favored more discrimination, not less.

President Dwight D. Eisenhower, who as a general had resisted segregation in the army, decided to just ignore the problem. Saying that "laws should not change people's hearts," he didn't take any action after a federal court ruled that the University of Alabama must accept Autherine Lucy as a student. The president's only response was, "I would certainly hope that we could avoid any interference." The university went right on enforcing its segregation policies.

Eisenhower was finally forced to take action one year later, in 1957, when under the watchful eye of national television cameras, Arkansas Governor Orville Faubus called out a unit of the National Guard to keep nine black youngsters from entering Central High School in Little Rock. Faced with a court order, he quickly called off the soldiers and sent the students home. When they came back a few days later, the school's entrance was blocked by a hostile mob that refused to give in to police efforts to move them out of the way. This time, Eisenhower himself called out the National Guard and sent in one thousand paratroopers as a backup. Even that didn't work. Governor Faubus simply closed down all the public schools in Little Rock and swore he'd never let them open again if they had to be integrated. The Supreme Court, meanwhile, put a deadline to its desegregation order and insisted on "immediate" integration, but Faubus stuck to his resolve and assumed the status of a savior of the South.

But blacks had already begun to fight fire with fire. When Rosa Parks, a black seamstress, was ordered to give up her seat on a public bus in Montgomery, Alabama, and was arrested for the crime, the local black community started a boycott of the local bus system on December 1, 1955. It didn't end until 382 days later, on December 21, 1956, when the transit authorities agreed to provide open seating on its buses.

Following that, Reverend Dr. Martin Luther King, Jr., began operating through the Student Nonviolent Coordinating Committee to organize "sit-ins," first in Montgomery and then all over the South to protest discrimination against blacks through local Jim Crow laws. They were eventually joined by concerned Northerners who shared the risk of arrest as well as physical and verbal abuse by challenging the local laws and sitting down at lunch counters and in hotels, public parks, churches—anywhere blacks were forbidden to show their faces. They also rented buses and staged "freedom rides," attracting angry white mobs along the way, and usually facing brutal treatment by the local police wherever they went.

The national spotlight turned on the problem in 1962, after a federal court ordered the University of Mississippi to admit James Meredith as its first black student. When he arrived for his first class, the state's governor, Ross Barnett was waiting there to block the door. Two days later, 320 federal marshals were sent there to make sure the door would be opened. President John F. Kennedy followed up with a nationally televised address appealing to Mississippi's sense of honor, but there seemed to be very little of that in evidence the next morning when the federal marshals were attacked with rocks, Molotov cocktails, and even bullets. The battle lasted all night. By morning, two were dead and nearly four hundred injured, nearly all of them U.S. marshals.

A few months later, in January 1963, Alabama Governor George C. Wallace announced in his inaugural address: "I draw the line in the dust and toss the gauntlet before the feet of tyranny. I say segregation now, segregation tomorrow, segregation forever."

Among the first to cross the line was Dr. Martin Luther King, Jr., who began campaigning for at least partial desegregation in Birmingham, Alabama, where there had been none at all. He and his fellow marchers were arrested and put behind bars almost as soon as they set foot on the street, and the following day other protest marchers were mowed down by fire hoses, attacked by police dogs, and moved along by cattle prods. President Kennedy negotiated a settlement that called for desegregation in Birmingham within ninety days, but his representatives had no sooner left town than bombs destroyed the home of Dr. King's younger brother, Reverend A. D. King, and the headquarters of his movement, which had been established in a local motel. That led to a violent black protest, and every minute of it was played out on national television. The public reacted with revulsion to images of unprecedented police brutality, and demonstrations against it broke out all over the country.

The hostility didn't seem to have an end. The day after Governor Wallace kept his promise to "stand at the schoolhouse door" to stop integration of the University of Alabama, the Birmingham Baptist Church was dynamited. A few days later Medgar Evers, a black activist, was gunned down in front of his own house. Soon afterward, President Kennedy proposed the strongest civil rights legislation in history, but it was still being debated when he was assassinated on November 22, 1963, and his successor, Lyndon B.Johnson, took up the cause.

Racial violence didn't stop while the debate was going on. In March, 1965, Dr. King organized a march from Selma, Alabama, to Montgomery to protest the arrest of two thousand blacks for the crime of trying to register to vote, and the shooting death of one of them who didn't seem to "know his place." Once again, television cameras were watching, and the scenes of marchers facing bull-whips, cattle prods, and clubs, prompted thousands from the North to go to Selma and join the march. President Johnson eventually provided Army troops for their protection and, although a northern clergyman had been beaten to death, there were no other serious incidents before the twenty thousand marchers finally reached Montgomery. However, a woman who had made the march was murdered on the way back.

A few months later, in August 1965, Congress passed a bill that guaranteed voting rights to all Americans, and President Johnson signed it into law. He had enacted President Kennedy's Civil Rights Act a year earlier, and as the South finally seemed to get the message, tensions began to cool down on both sides. Racial integration was still far from universal, but the commitment was there.

During the years this racial violence was stalking the South, military bases, heavily concentrated in the region, were like islands of tranquility. Men and women of both races lived and worked together behind the fences that surrounded them; they shared equally in all the recreational facilities, they shared living quarters, and even went to school together. But the towns and cities outside the gates were like another world. Restaurants and bars refused to serve blacks, they couldn't share taxis or sit together on buses with white servicepersons, and even off-base USO clubs were strictly segregated.

Military personnel might have been able to shrug off the restrictions simply by not venturing off the base, but many of them lived off-base, especially the growing number of black officers. Quarters for officers and their families within military installations are always in short supply, and more often than not during the 1950s and early 1960s, blacks found themselves at the bottom of the list for months and even years because of "gentlemen's agreements" that ignored the rules requiring equal treatment. When they went outside looking for housing, the doors were usually closed to them. The situation wasn't limited to the South. As far north as Brunswick, Maine, black airmen from the nearby Topsham Air Force Base were routinely turned away by local real estate agents, a pattern that was repeated in a great many northern towns and cities where local residents were worried about the effect on real estate values if they allowed blacks to live in their neighborhoods.

In spite of their policies of equality, none of the services enforced them when they signed contracts with local landlords for housing their personnel, leaving it up to the property owners themselves to "operate in conformity" with local custom. The housing referral staffs of most military facilities usually refused to list properties that wouldn't allow pets or children, but almost never refused to offer those that were closed to blacks. As one location officer explained it, that would virtually eliminate their lists of available housing.

Black officers and enlisted men who had children faced a similar nightmare. Just as the military bases had been integrated, the schools on them did away with color bars, too. But posts that had their own schools were few and far between. As a practical matter, black servicemen and women were forced to send their children to schools in the local community. Most of these black youngsters—notwithstanding the momentous 1954 Supreme Court decision—were still attending substandard segregated schools that were usually much further away from home than newer schools that had been built with federal funds, due to the impact of the large number of military dependents in the area. Yet these schools were still closed to blacks by local rules. The government didn't step in to correct the situation until 1963, when it reached the conclusion that segregated schools weren't "suitable," and announced that it would withhold funding from those that denied education to blacks. It still didn't solve the problem, although about two dozen school districts complied, because the ruling applied only to children who lived on military reservations. And because almost 90 percent of black dependents lived outside the gates, the government went right on funding and subsidizing segregated schools, and it continued to do so until 1964, when the new Civil Rights law went into effect.

The war in Vietnam had its beginnings in 1955, when U.S. advisers were sent to Saigon to help the South Vietnamese government, in its fight against Ho Chi Minh's Communist Vietminh rebels. It officially began four years later when the first casualties were reported among the advisers. It would become the longest war in American history, and the first in which blacks and whites fought together as true equals.

The war escalated and became a fact of American life, in mid–1964, when Congress passed the Gulf of Tonkin Resolution in response to an unsubstantiated report that North Vietnamese patrol boats had fired on U.S. Navy vessels. It empowered President Johnson to "take all measures to repel any armed attack against the United States." In fact, the president had already taken the measure of ordering air strikes against the North. The United States was now engaged in a full-fledged shooting war.

By that point, a combination of steady volunteering and strong reenlistment numbers had brought the number of blacks in the military up to nearly 12 percent, about equal to their proportion in the overall population. They served in every capacity, and earned high praise everywhere they served. Pentagon officials were generally as proud as new fathers, and it was just about impossible to find anyone there who would admit that he had ever been against military integration.

Then something began to happen to the numbers, The draft was bringing in black recruits in larger percentages than whites. By 1967, 64 percent of registered blacks had been caught in the Selective Service net, compared to 31 percent of whites. There were several reasons why it worked out that way. More potential white draftees were being rejected for medical reasons, and many more were able to get deferments as students or because of their involvement in occupations that were considered important to the war effort. Many, of course, also slipped across the border into Canada and out of reach of their draft boards. Young white men were also better able to join ROTC programs, and large numbers of them joined the National Guard, crossing their fingers that their units wouldn't be called up. Almost none were, as it turned out, because President Johnson had decided for political reasons to fight the war with regular recruits and not by activating national guard and reserve units. The 369th Regiment in Harlem was among those units that were not sent to Vietnam.

The Pentagon lowered its educational standards in 1966, and then went back through the list of rejected draftees, claiming that the move was intended to allow young blacks to get an education in the military that they had missed in substandard segregated schools. Over the next three years, the prgram known as Project One Hundred Thousand, brought almost 200,000 draftees into the service. Some 80 percent of them were high-school dropouts, and 40 percent were blacks. Over one-third of them were discharged before their enlistments expired, in most cases on charges of desertion. Responding to the Defense Department's initial announcement that the program was intended to "give these men . . . a sense of personal achievent, a sense of succeeding at some task, a sense of their own intrinsic potential," they more often than not referred to themselves as "the moron corps," and the officers whose job it was to train them seemed to agree. The Pentagon preferred to call them "New Standards Men," but the net effect was a lowering of standards. Looking back on it in 1996, President Bill Clinton, who himself had received a student deferment back then, admitted that "the best and brightest did not go to Vietnam." At the time the Pentagon decided to recruit less than the best, the *Baltimore Sun* reported that the net effect of such policies was that "the ghetto man's education points him to the rice paddies."

Indeed, it did seem as though this was a war being fought almost exclusively by black troops, but the numbers tell a different story. According to Defense Department statistics, covering all of the years of the war, and released after it ended in 1973, more than 8.7 million U.S. troops served there, and slightly less than 10 percent of them were African-Americans, although blacks of military age accounted for about 13.5 percent of the population at the time. Over the nearly ten years of actual fighting in Vietnam, blacks accounted for slightly less than 11 percent of the Americans involved in combat, while of the total dead, 12.5 percent were blacks. Whites accounted for more than 88 percent of the Vietnam fighting force over the same period, and they represented almost 87 percent of the ones who died there. Compared to previous wars, black participation—and death—were significantly higher in Vietnam. The difference, though, was not that blacks had been relegated to serve as "cannon fodder," but that they had never been so completely free to fight for their country in such large numbers. This was also the first time the American public had been able to see actual combat on the television news, and they were shaken by the sight of black faces in nearly every encounter, giving a general impression that Vietnam was a black man's war.

The key element in the difference between the Defense Department's final report and statistical snapshots that were issued at various stages while the war was in progress was that the previously high rate of black reenlistments began to drop off in the late 1960s. By 1970, more than 87 percent of blacks were opting to leave the service when they had the chance. It was an entirely new phenomenon. In the mid–1960s, the reenlistment rate among blacks had been as high as 46 percent.

Despite the reluctance of many of them to re-up, the black men doing the fighting and dying in Southeast Asia didn't appear to believe that they were shouldering more than their share of the risk. The *New York Times* noted: "The American ground forces are almost free of racial tension, and most soldiers—Negro and white—appear proud of this." But as people were starting to say on American college campuses, the times they were a-changin'.

Back home, the war had started to dominate the news at a time when the domestic fight for universal civil rights was still unfinished. Most black leaders were well aware of the great victory that military integration represented, but they were also opposed to the Vietnam War on moral grounds, as many Americans were. Although they had been fighting for generations for the right of black Americans to fight in their country's wars, to many this particular war didn't seem to them to be worth the taking of a single life, white or black.

Black activist members of the Student Nonviolent Coordinating Committee, the Congress of Racial Equality, and Dr. Martin Luther King's Southern Christian Leadership Conference had all come out strongly against the war, and their speeches and demonstrations gave the impression that Vietnam had degenerated into a war between the black and yellow races, of which some wanted no part. Reverend Andrew Young of the SCLC said that their opposition stemmed from their belief that "this war is blowing up our future." Dr. King criticized:

> We are taking the young black men who have been crippled by our society and sending them eight thousand miles away to guarantee the liberties in Southeast Asia which they have not found in Southwest Georgia and East Harlem. So we have been faced with the cruel irony of watching Negro and white boys on TV screens as they kill and die together for a nation that has been unable to seat them together in the same school. So we watch them in brutal solidarity burning the huts of a poor village, but we realize that they could never live together on the same block in Detroit.

The *New York Times* noted in 1967: "This is the first time in the history of America that national Negro figures are not urging black youths to take up arms in support of American policy to improve the lot of the black man in the United States."

Malcolm X of the Nation of Islam, was actually urging them to actively oppose being sent to Vietnam: "The United States is the most hypocritical government since the world began. It's supposed to be a democracy, supposed to be for freedom and all that kind of stuff when they want to draft you and put you in the Army and send you to Saigon to fight for them—and then you've got to turn around and all night long discuss how you're going to get the right to register to vote without getting murdered."

The Black Panther party was also calling for young blacks to fight for their rights at home and not for somebody else's rights on a different continent. The organization even demanded: "We want all black men to be exempt from military service." Stokeley Carmichael, the head of the Student Nonviolent Coordinating

Committee, added fuel to the fire by making speeches across the country promoting "Black Power," and galvanized even previously nonmilitant young black people. He got even more attention by coining the powerful phrase, "Hell no, we won't go!" which quickly became the new cry for many young whites as well as blacks.

The movement also had a strong impact on the men who had already gone into the war, as the rising tide of militancy at home started to have an effect on the military abroad. While black soldiers had kept up the drumbeat for equality in the service almost continually since the Revolutionary War, they started to ask for something more in the 1960s. Although they were finally being treated the same as whites, they started to ask for recognition of their unique culture as well.

It wasn't a one-sided reaction. There had been pockets of resentment among white soldiers since the war began, but it intensified in the wake of news from home that their fellow Americans, and black leaders in particular, were not only agitating for an end to the war, but seemed to be questioning the patriotism of the men who were fighting in it.

Colin Powell, who served as a brigade commander of the Second Infantry Division in Vietnam, was caught in the middle of the problem:

> The whites wanted rock and country and western. The blacks wanted soul, Aretha Franklin and Dionne Warwick. The issue got so testy that we summoned the Tong Di Chong [the nearest town to the base] bar owners to see if we could work out a fair formula. They finally agreed that they would feature roughly seven "white" songs for every three "black" songs. As a result of this compromise, the whites were unhappy only thirty percent of the time, and the blacks seventy percent.

The men under him simply divided the town in half with a line running down the middle that they called "the crack." It was whites on one side and blacks on the other until Powell's CO ordered him to patrol the town with MPs to break up any racial incidents and wipe out that symbolic crack. Powell wrote: "We half expected him to say, 'Racism will end at zero seven hundred tomorrow morning.'" Surprisingly, the plan worked, but there weren't enough such simple solutions to bring an end to racism in Vietnam, short of a pullout.

When Dr. Martin Luther King, Jr. was assassinated on April 4, 1968, the entire country erupted in violence. As bloody demonstrations raged in more than a hundred American cities, it extended to military bases around the world, too. The strongest reaction took place in Vietnam itself where whites paraded in Ku Klux Klan robes at Que Viet, Confederate flags were raised over the base at Da Nang, and a burning cross appeared in front of navy headquarters at Cam Ranh Bay. The military responded by banning Confederate flags from all bases and organizing committees to watch for and report racial incidents, but it was already too late. The close-knit buddy system that had been a source of military pride had begun to deteriorate. No amount of flag banning or disciplinary action could close the gap that had been forced open.

The Pentagon knew it was facing a serious morale problem in Vietnam, but they had an even bigger one back home. When troops at Fort Hood, Texas, staged a demonstration protesting their assignment to Chicago, where they would be used as shock troops against protests anticipated at the 1968 Democratic National Convention, its leaders were court-martialed. As that incident was being defused, a white noncommissioned officer was killed by blacks serving under him at the Camp Lejeune U.S. Marine base in North Carolina , and in retaliation, a hail of phosphorus grenades burned the home of a retired black marine who was living on the base.

Blacks and whites at Fort Jackson, South Carolina, joined together as "GIs United Against the War in Vietnam" in the late 1960s, but they were refused permission to hold any meetings on the post. Nine of them were confined to their barracks, in fact, and six were discharged as "undesirables." It led to an official restatement, issued to army personnel around the world, of what had been army policy all along: "servicemen have limited rights to possess written material, attend off-post meetings, join servicemen's unions, publish papers off post, make complaints, and petition for redress of grievances." In other words, it had all been a misunderstanding. While such rights are guaranteed by the Constitution's First Amendment, military personnel sign away many of their civilian rights in their enlistment agreements.

The misunderstanding went unnoticed by black troops in Vietnam, though. They had long since taken to sporting "Afro" haircuts and "solidarity" wristbands. They adopted "Black Power" salutes and "dap" handshakes. According to a black soldier interviewed by *Newsweek* magazine, the handshakes, also called "soul shakes," began innocently enough. "In the beginning, you know, we used to dap quietly on the side. But then, wow, it looked like it annoyed some of the white guys. So the idea got around to dap a litle louder, do it a little more." Their officers were told to ignore all the attempts on the part of their men to assert their culture, in the interest of keeping anger to a minimum. The integrated military was degenerating into the kind of segregation that had dogged the services for most of their history. But this time, it was the black troops themselves that were doing the segregating.

In a report on what it called an army in evolution, *Life* magazine reported: "Old ideas of dress, behavior, discipline and rank no longer apply. . . . Virtually no draftee wants to be fighting in Vietnam anyway, and in return for his reluctant participation he demands, and gets personal freedoms that would have driven a

MacArthur or a Patton apoplectic. . . . All questions—including 'Why?'—are permissible."

The military itself regarded all this as a temporary situation, and it began making plans to turn things around. The first shot came in 1971 with a survey concluding that what was happening in Vietnam was going to lead to a breakdown of the army's "moral strength" in the long term. Among the men who was assigned to do something about it was Major Colin Powell, who had recently been assigned to the Pentagon after his tour of duty in Vietnam. His mandate was to "take a couple of bright guys and start rethinking the unthinkable." He was facing an uphill battle.

In the meantime, the Defense Department had formed an Inter-service Task Force on Education in Race Relations, and base commanders began instituting such educational programs as seminars and open discussions. Post libraries were stocked with books on black history, and post newspapers published articles on black culture. The drive was extended to training programs for military barbers and beauticians in the art of styling black people's hair; sprays to maintain them began appearing on PX shelves, where black personnel could also buy dashikis, books and cards with "soul" themes, and phonograph records by black musical groups. They even found some fare resembling soul food available in the mess halls.

But the attempt was less than successful. If anything, it seemed to widen the gulf between blacks and whites, who refused to interact with one another unless it was absolutely necessary. Many of the blacks the program had been devised to accommodate brushed it all off as an attempt at 'brainwashing." In the midst of it all, a movement emerged on bases in Europe to encourage blacks to bond together and mount formal protests against perceived injustices. By the early 1970s, an officer stationed in West Germany complained,

"Race is my problem—not the Russians, not Vietnam, Jordan, nor maneuvers. I just worry about keeping my troops—black and white—from getting at one another."

A Defense Department survey of black troops stationed in Europe, released in 1970, reported that blacks were generally opposed to fighting what they called "a white man's war." It said that they believed, "their place was back in the States where they could fight to liberate and free their black brothers and sisters from the dirty, stinky teeming ghettos and from all forms of racial bigotry and oppression." The survey, which had been conducted by Frank Render, the Deputy Assistant Secretary of Defense for Equal Opportunity, and the Pentagon's highest-ranking African-American, concluded that the problem stemmed from a breakdown in command leadership, and recommended that human relations councils should be established in every major command.

The greatest leap forward came from Admiral Elmo R. Zumwalt, who became Chief of Naval Operations in 1970. Even though it had once characterized itself as the most color-blind of the the services, the navy was still dragging its feet on full integration, twenty-two years after President Truman's order to put it into effect "as rapidly as possible," and Zumwalt was dismayed at the lack of equality he found in his command. He immediately announced that he was going to do away with "the lily-white racist Navy," and found himself knee-deep in opposition from Congress, from senior naval officers, and from his predecesor, Admiral Thomas Moorer, who publicly accused him of "blackening" the service.

But Zumwalt was the man in charge by then, and he stuck to his resolve, saying that he believed "there is no black Navy, no white Navy, just one Navy—the United States Navy." He ordered black personnel assigned to its recruiting stations, and approved a new advertising campaign promising potential recruits, "You can be black and Navy, too." And then he went to work to keep the promise. He issued an all-hands memo that ordered everyone, from seamen to admirals, to, "help seek out and eliminate those demeaning areas of discrimination that plague our minority shipmates. . . . Ours must be a Navy family that recognizes no artifical barriers of race, color, or religion."

In a barrage of similar memos that sailors began calling "Z-grams," he ordered mandatory sensitivity training at all levels, and let it be known that he expected blacks to be trained for, and promoted to, better jobs and higher ranks. Among the changes he instituted was the end of long-standing rules against sideburns, mustaches, and beards, and those requiring enlisted personnel to wear uniforms all the time, even when they were off duty.

Zumwalt also lowered the educational standards for new recruits, eliminating the stumbling block that the navy had set up back when integration had first been ordered. It extended its ROTC program to black universities and colleges, and history was made at the U.S. Naval Academy in 1972 when 132 African-Americans entered Annapolis as naval cadets. During the previous year, Captain Samuel S. Gravely, Jr., had become the first black admiral in the history of the U.S. Navy, and twelve of its ships were commanded by African-Americans. They had come a long way from the days when they appeared to be doomed to make their navy careers in the Steward Service.

Not long after Zumwalt took over as Chief of Naval Operations, he scheduled a series of meetings in Washington with his senior officers and African-American personnel that, significantly, also included their wives. It turned out to be much more than lip service. The admiral's report to the Secretary of the Navy said: "From this group of Navy men and their wives, we learned of discrimination of an order we had no idea existed. We didn't even understand the nature or the basis of some of it until we listened to this group. Since then I have seen the transformation not only in myself, but in all those senior personnel who were in the room on this occasion."

Zumwalt's memos and speeches attracted reams of press attention, and it was inevitable that it would get attention in the halls of Congress, where the chairman of the House Armed Services Committee, Edward Hebert of Louisiana, called for an investigation in 1972 to look into what he called the navy's "*alleged* racial and disciplinary problems." It was a secret investigation, of course, but Congressman Hebert found himself the subject of press scrutiny, too, along with his conclusion that there wasn't any racism in the Navy, but that its problems came from excessive permissiveness in allowing blacks to qualify for commissions. This was an assertion that few newspaper readers or television viewers would let pass without an argument. It was the last time the Southern delegation in Congress made any attempt to get in the way of military desegregation.

The navy was not alone in working to clean up its act. Although the war in Vietnam had ended by then, the United States was still in a state of high alert as it continued to face the threat of a possible nuclear war with Russia. But the troops coming home from Southeast Asia were demoralized in ways that the American military had never been before. Many soldiers had become heroin addicts, and the majority of them, blacks and whites alike, were harboring negative views on race that hadn't been as glaringly out in the open since the days of Reconstruction after the Civil War. President Richard M. Nixon said in a private staff meeting that he believed it would take five hundred years to turn things around. But he—and everyone else in authority—knew that they didn't have the luxury of time.

At the end of 1969 Secretary of Defense Melvin H. Laird issued guidelines for an equal opportunity program called "Directive 1100.15," which ordered the Pentagon to implement affirmative action programs immediately, and to begin developing plans that would make equal opportunity the centerpiece of all military operations. The directive also demanded that base commanders close their gates to civilian contractors as well as any other outside organizations that didn't support equal opportunity.

Eighteen months later, in June 1971, Laird issued another order known as "Directive 1322.11," which established new educational policies. Among its creations was the Defense Race Relations Institute, which was charged with the responsibility of increasing understanding of ethnic differences and leading the way to racial harmony.

The institute, which was based at Patrick Air Force Base in Florida, had to start from scratch; but in less than a year, it had produced materials and educational techniques that not only served the military establishment, but were adopted by civilian schools and businesses as well. The instructors that the institute trained fanned out to their own branches of the service, and eventually, every American military installation around the world was giving mandatory race-relations training to both officers and enlisted personnel.

Among the required reading in these courses was "Understanding the Minority Member in Uniform," a text that addressed the problem of African-American Vietnam veterans:

A black in uniform does not cease to be black. Like any other serviceman, he seeks to retain his personal and racial identity while identifying and relating to the service.

For generations, the black American has perceived himself to be without identity. Personal success was usually achieved by accommodating and imitating whites; therefore, the black was expected to conform and act as if he were invisible and inferior.

The younger generation of blacks wishes to be considered equal without being different. Thus, the logical emergence of a thurst for identity. The young black serviceman strongly desires and needs the opportunity to express his views with young whites and with older black NCOs and officers. He has seen the injustices in the nation's schools, courts, and law-enforcement agencies, and in his quest for economic security. Consequently, he is socially aware and sensitive to any form of discrimination, real or imagined. Due to the social patterns in the society from which he emerged, he frequently maintains close relations with his black brothers, resulting in voluntary polarization. Some young blacks consider violence an acceptable course of action for resolving conflict.

. . . The average young black serviceman resents having his newly found racial pride confused and interpreted as evidence that he is a black militant or a racist. He realizes that the new problem facing the service is protecting him and his white comrades from the influence of the black and white racist. This point is extremely important because the increase in aggressiveness and vocalism of the black servicemen is not necessarily a problem. It only becomes a problem when commanders overreact and write off these blacks as troublemakers and militants.

What made such texts remarkable was not so much their approach, which was revolutionary at the time, but that they represented official military policy and that absorbing and obeying them was mandatory for every man and woman, every officer, NCO and enlisted person in every branch of the service. Before long, it became as basic to the military experience as basic training itself.

All of the services rallied to the program, although they were well aware that recruits, African-American as well as white, brought along attitudes they had grown up with, and that the equal opportunity and educational programs did not work like magic wands.

*   *   *

Most of the studies of returning Vetnam vets concluded that the Selective Service System had been the real villain. Most African-Americans among the returnees believed that they had been drafted far out of proportion to their numbers at home, and that draft boards gave unfair deferments to the whites on their lists. They were also convinced that the antiwar activists back home had been not so much opposed to the war as they were to their own status as draft bait; perhaps, many black soldiers reasoned, they were successful at avoiding doing time in the service because the Pentagon wasn't interested in drafting political militants.

President Richard M. Nixon pledged to end the draft, and in 1969 he formed a commission to study ways to accomplish it. At the same time, he amended the existing law to turn it into a lottery system that was based on birth dates, rather than relying on individual draft boards to fill quotas based on their own local standards. The new draft law also did away with several of the previous reasons for automatic deferment, including college enrollment. When the modified law went into effect at the end of 1971, it became known as "Vietnam Bingo," because anybody whose number came up wound up wearing a uniform.

The president's commission reached the conclusion that military patriotism would be compromised if it didn't include a cross section of all Americans, and, worse, it was in danger of being staffed by soldiers of fortune and young men who were unemployable elsewhere. But it still strongly supported an all-volunteer force, which it perceived would better-serve the country than a military of conscripts and volunteers.

The Defense Department bought into the idea. Secretary Laird said, "We do not foresee any difference between the racial composition of the all-volunteer force and the racial composition of the Nation. . . .We are determined that the all-volunteer force shall have a broad appeal to young men and women of all racial, ethnic and economic backgrounds."

The last draftee reported for duty on June 30, 1973, and every recruit that has followed in his footsteps since that day has been a volunteer. The military had become America's biggest equal-opportunity employer.

It began to compete with the private sector for young high school and college graduates by increasing pay levels and making military life generally more attractive. In spite of the Defense Secretary Laird's conviction that the new military would represent a cross section of America, blacks were the first to realize that they were being offered a good deal. In the last year of the draft, they represented 12.6 percent of all enlisted personnel, and during the first decade of the volunteer force, the ratio jumped to 22.1 percent. During the same period, the percentage of black officers almost doubled, and by the mid–1980s, there were thirty-three black top line officers in the military services. Secretary of the Army Clifford L. Alexander was an African-American.

As the new military was gearing up, black history and race-relations study were not only required courses, in basic training programs across the services, as inevitable as push-ups, but intensive study was required of the officers and NCOs who would be leading them. Their understanding and commitment to these studies were scrutinized and made part of the proficiency reports that became part of the files following them throughout their military careers. These reports are crucial to any hope of promotion, and one result of the policy was more promotions among African-Americans. At the same time, officers whose efficiency reports contained even a hint of racism were ususally relieved of their commands. If the offense was considered serious enough, they could expect to find themselves looking for new jobs in the private sector. The policy has been intensified in the years since it was first instituted, and in today's military it is a rare officer, commissioned or noncommissioned, who isn't sensitive to the issue of race. It has become second nature to them, not something they need to keep reminding themselves of, somewhat like remembering to salute a superior officer, black or white.

Considering the high rate of black discontent in its ranks at the end of the Vietnam era, the Pentagon was surprised at first by the seeming eagerness of African-Americans to join up for the volunteer service. The rate hasn't diminished in recent decades. By the dawn of the new millennium, three out of every ten army personnel were black, and the ratio was nearly as high in the other services, too. In 2001, less than thirty years after the draft was phased out in 1973, more than one-third of all staff sergeants and first sergeants in the army were African-Americans, and white enlistees were virtually guaranteed the prospect of taking orders from a black NCO at some point during their active duty career. Equal opportunity aside, economics had everything to do with it.

Even without other benefits and bonuses, recruits in the lowest ranks of the military, such as an army buck private or a navy seaman, earns $1,200 a month, with a guarantee of a raise every year. At the current minimum wage, a high-school graduate can expect to earn only half that much. On top of that, almost no private employers offer free housing, free meals, free clothing, and free medical care, not to mention the longer vacations offered by the military, plus the opportunity to retire after twenty years with better-than-average veterans' benefits. A black enlistee entering the service at the age of eighteen could be free to begin a second career at the age of thirty-eight, and would often have a background of experience with cutting-edge technology that opens up all kinds of previously undreamed-of job possibilities, a classic win-win situation.

But the biggest boon of all for young African-Americans in the new military is the opportunity to get a college education. After World War II, the G.I. Bill of Rights paid college costs for a whole

generation of veterans, and it was reinstated in 1985 to give
Vietnam veterans and members of the all-volunteer military the
same benefits. The new programs also allow service members to
accumulate college credits through their regular training and on-
the-job experience.

All of these new perks, added to more enlightened attitudes on
racial matters, makes all those years of black demands for the right
to serve their country seem far more than worthwhile.

But the right to serve also brings the right to go into combat which,
although it had been a major demand by black leaders from the
start, lost some of its luster when African-Americans began dying in
battle. Now some of those same black leaders were beginning to
worry that, considering their increased numbers, African-American
troops were going to be facing battlefield casualties far out of proportion to their percentage of the population. Of course, what was
lost in the argument was the fact that everyone who served, regardless of race, was in uniform by choice, and that the risks are the
result of that choice.

The fact that everybody who was in the service was there because
it was where they chose to be, for one reason or another, had a dramatic calming effect on racial incidents on military installations,
and the Department of Defense was constantly fine-tuning its interracial communications programs to eliminate any pockets of protest
that might still exist. By mid–1981, it issued what it called "The
Charter of Human Goals," setting new, unprecedented standards
that became the military's official policy:

In all that we do, we must show respect for the serviceman, the
servicewoman, and civilian employees recognizing their individual needs, aspirations, and capabilities.

The defense of the nation requires a well-trained force, military and civilian, regular and reserve. To provide such a force, we must increase the attractiveness of a career in Defense so that the service member and the civilian employee will feel the highest pride in themselves and their work, in the uniform and military profession.

The attainment of these goals requres that we strive:

- To attract to the defense service people with ability, dedication, and capacity for growth;
- To provide opportunity for everyone, military and civilian, to rise to as high a level of responsibility as possible, dependent only on individual talent and diligence;
- To make military and civilian service in the Department of Defense a model of equal opportunity for all, regardless of race, color, sex, religion, or national origin and to hold all those who do business with the Department to full compliance with the policy of equal employment opportunity;
- To help each service member in leaving the service to readjust to civilian life; and
- To contribute to the improvement of our society, including its disadvantaged members, by greater utilization of our human and physical resources while maintaining full effectiveness in the performance of our primary duties.

The United States had vaulted light-years ahead from the day when Henry Johnson, Needham Roberts, and their fellow Harlem Hellfighters arrived in France back in 1918, and from that night in 1775, when blacks and whites joined together to answer Paul Revere's warning. For the first time in its history, the United States military is seamlessly united at last.

The first test of this new united military came late in 1983, two years after the Human Goals Charter was issued, when U.S. troops invaded the Caribbean island of Grenada in what was called "Operation Fury." It was billed as an effort to rescue American medical students on the island after it had been taken over by a Cuban-led Communist government. But the real issue was the landing of Russian weaponry there, and the construction of a new airport, with the hint that there was more to come.

It was far from America's finest hour. Some landing assaults were misdirected, helicopters crashed into one another, and after an almost daylong siege of a barracks building, the American troops were embarrassed to discover that it had been been empty all along. Still, the action was over in just a few days, and it was pronounced a success. As was fitting for America's new military, there were no figures released on the racial makeup of the invasion force. The distinction simply wasn't being addressed any longer.

In another six years, in 1989, U.S. forces went into combat again, this time in Panama where the goal was to overthrow the government of dictator Manuel Noriega, supervise a democratic election, and disarm Panama's defenses. Apparently the American troops had learned a great deal in the intervening years, and the so-called "Operation Just Cause" was smooth, professional, and effective. Once again, the military didn't issue any figures revealing racial breakdowns, and the television camera crews, which were even more ubiquitous in Panama than they had been in Vietnam, didn't make any efforts to single out any of the African-Americans who were involved.

During the Persian Gulf War, the new military proved itself, and finally wiped away the stigma of Vietnam. The war was mounted in response to Iraq's invasion of Kuwait. As General Colin Powell, the

Chairman of the Joint Chiefs of Staff at the time, put it, "We have given America a clear win at low casualties in a noble cause, and the American people fell in love again with their armed forces." This time, the Department of Defense did release racial statistics, and it revealed that about 20 percent of the troops who went to the Persian Gulf were African-Americans, representing less than 12 percent of the population of America in the early 1990s.

Other figures the Defense Department released revealed the nature of America's new military, beyond racial makeup. Ninety-five percent of them were high-school graduates, compared to a 75 percent U.S. average. The incidence of drug and alcohol problems, bane of the military in previous eras, was nearly nonexistent. The percentage of married men and women was higher than in any previous American fighting force, the majority professed religious beliefs, and the average age was higher than had ever been seen before in an American fighting force, an indication that the volunteer military was also attracting more recruits who were expecting to make a career of military service.

By the time the Gulf War ended, after forty-three days of air action and another hundred hours of fighting on the ground, the Americans had lost 182 dead, 15 percent of them black. The numbers prompted a Scripps-Howard News Service article that appeared in newspapers around the world: "Another expert prediction fell victim to facts the other day: Expectations that black soldiers would do a heavy proportion of the dying in the Gulf War turned out to be wrong. . . . In any case, it's important to remember that the 182 American troops who died were black, white or Hispanic only secondarily. First and foremost, they were all Americans."

Although National Guard units hadn't been activated during the Vietnam War, more than 53,000 Guardsmen saw service in the

Persian Gulf, and among them was the 719th Transportation Company, which had been formed out of the 369th Infantry Regiment. Like the original Hellfighters, they were the first to arrive on the scene ready for action (they were already there when the fighting broke out), and they were assigned to support the 101st Air Assault Division, based in Saudi Arabia. Unlike most of the fully integrated army, the regiment was still essentially an all-black outfit, but with a healthy percentage of Hispanics, reflecting the changing makeup of the neighborhood back home in Harlem. They established a home away from home out there in the Arabian desert that they called "Guardian City," honoring the black organization of police officers known as the Guardians, to which many of them belonged. There were also New York City firefighters, subway workers, sanitation workers, teachers, and city employees among them, and the unit also included twelve women enlisted personnel and one female officer. Their job was driving tractor-trailer rigs across the desert to deliver supplies and heavy equipment up to the front lines.

After the war was declared over, the 719th Transportation Company was broken up, and its personnel assigned to frontline divisions, although they had not been trained in combat operations. Even though more combat seemed unlikely at that stage, their families back home mounted a strong protest with the Defense Department. "They should not be out there in the desert at their age [their average age was forty]," said the protesters, "They are weekend warriors who are not prepared to be in a ground war. It's almost like suicide." A representative of the 369th Regiment Veterans' Association wrote them off as "troublemakers," and the military itself brushed them off by saying: "National Guard units, like any other Army units, wherever they must go to perform their unit missions." The bottom line was that the heirs to the Hellfighter tradition were the first on the scene in the Persian Gulf, and they were among the last to leave.

In mid-January 1991, two months after the National Guard company from Harlem arrived in the Gulf region, the air defensive actions, which had been know as Operation Desert Shield, changed to a ground offensive and was given the new designation Operation Desert Storm. Before the first day ended, all of the Iraqi missile sites had been declared destroyed. The strategy beyond that was to attack the enemy's supply lines, factories and depots. Colin Powell, who had been deeply involved in the advance planning, said of the Iraqi army. "Our strategy is very simple. First we are going to cut it off, and then we are going to kill it." Considering that the Bush White House had ordered that the war couldn't last more than one hundred hours, the strategy appeared to be perfect. The coalition forces captured almost 70,000 prisoners—so many, in fact, that there weren't enough trucks to carry them back behind the lines. The ground troops just disarmed the Iraqis who gave up and then sent them walking in a generally southern direction. In the course of the operation, which involved an estimated 468,000 Americans, 148 were killed in the fighting, and 467 were wounded. The enemy lost more than 100,000 killed, and 300,000 wounded, and much of their country's infrastructure had been seriously destroyed.

Colin Powell joined Norman Schwarzkopf, the commander of Desert Storm, in a victorious ticker-tape parade up New York's lower Broadway in June 1991. It was the first time since Henry Johnson rode up Fifth Avenue in an open car back in 1919 that New York had opened its heart to its own homegrown African-American hero.

Despite Colin Powell's having become a bona fide national hero, he was about to become the focus of a new controversy. Twenty years earlier, when he had been asked to "take a group of bright guys and start rethinking the unthinkable," what they were looking for was a way to cut the size of the armed forces. What Powell and his bright guys came up with was what they called a new "Base Army," but the idea seemed to be ahead of its time. Its time finally came in the form of Powell's "Strategic Overview: 1994," projecting the military's needs over the next four years, which combined his original Base Army concept with some new wrinkles.

His concept was based on the belief that the new Base Army needed to be more mobile than any army of the past. He called for preparation for warfare with an Atlantic command made up of aircraft and armored battalions, and a combined Pacific force of U.S. Navy, Air Force, and Army units along with a contingency force prepared to deal with Third World brushfire operations. Although the Soviet threat had virtually disappeared, he said he believed that Korea, the Philippines, and the Persian Gulf region would be the flash points for any near-term U.S. involvement.

Powell's new plan was drafted in response to a congressional demand for across- the-board-cuts in military spending of $10–$14 billion. That meant that bases would have to be closed, personnel numbers cut, ROTC units eliminated, recruitment advertising reduced, and even some veterans' benefits done away with. As the largest of the services, the army would feel the greatest pinch. The active-duty force of the combined services was slated to be reduced from 2.1 million to 1.6 million, and the army alone stood to be reduced from 1.65 million to about 520,000. Its advertising budget had already been cut by some $17 million before the personnel cuts were scheduled to kick in.

The proposed cuts brought protests on both sides of the racial divide. A senior black army officer predicted: "Conservatively, sixty thousand blacks will be discharged during the next year or two," and he wondered aloud what was going to become of them.

Another black officer demanded, "Save the boys, not the toys," and noted: "As we close out this century, we'll have invisible bombers to clobber invisible enemies, new nuclear missiles galore and more high-tech subs, ships, planes, and Star Wars goodies, too. . . . As usual the wrong stuff for most probable wars. . . . The world's mightiest military power was defeated [in Vietnam] by troops that were light on hardware, but heavy on guts and know-how."

In general, the public was in favor of the cuts. Depending on their point of view, it represented new savings to reduce taxes, or to finish the job of bringing blacks into the American mainstream. The military, of course, was not at all pleased with the idea, and the *New York Times* helped state their case in a news analysis that asked, "What does the nation lose if the military no longer serves as a channel for upward mobility for those at the bottom of the social ladder?"

By 1996, the cuts that were made reduced the army by eight combat divisions, the air force by a dozen fighter wings, and the navy by ninety-four ships. The military was ultimately reduced by 36 percent, with a surprising lack of pain because a great deal of the cutting of personnel came through early retirements. Unlike the business world, where downsizing is usually accomplished on a "last hired, first fired," basis, the military was more surgical in its cuts, and promising young blacks, who would have been automatically eliminated in the private sector, managed to stay on their upward path.

The cuts had almost no effect on black enlistments. By the time the troop reductions ended, African-Americans accounted for nearly 22 percent of the active-duty forces, and the number has stayed consistent over the years since.

By the beginning of the twenty-first century, the U.S. Army had about 495,000 men and women on its payroll. Among its male officers, slightly more than 10 percent were African-Americans, and almost 21 percent of the females in the officer corps were black. Together, the numbers represent an increase of 5 percent over the previous twenty years, and the trend is still holding steady. When the Harlem Hellfighters went to France in 1918, African-American army officers were as uncommon as blacks in southern governor's mansions.

Although blacks in the military's officer corps still fall below percentages represented in the overall population, the black people serving under them fall well above the statistics. According to Census 2000, 12.3 percent of Americans are African-Americans.

Today, military opportunities for blacks are something most of us take for granted. But it didn't just happen. It is the legacy that goes back more than two hundred years, through the efforts of thousands of blacks who have fought for the right to serve their country.

Colin Powell, one of the men who fought hardest for that right, wrote in his autobiography: "The Army was living the democratic ideal ahead of the rest of America. Beginning in the fifties, less discrimination, a truer merit system, and leveler playing fields existed inside the gates of our military posts than in any southern city hall or northern corporation. The Army, therefore, made it easier for me to love my country, with all its flaws, and to serve her with all my heart."

POSTSCRIPT

The 15th New York Negro Regiment of Infantry was formed on June 2, 1913 and was officially merged into the New York National Guard on June 29, 1916. It was mustered into the U.S. Army on July 25, 1917, when it was redesignated the 369th Infantry Regiment of the 93rd Division.

The regiment was sent to France on March 1, 1918, where it was attached to the French Fourth Army. Two of its men, Henry Johnson and Needham Roberts were the first Americans to earn France's highest honor, the Croix de Guerre, for their heroic predawn action in subduing a German patrol on May 14, 1918. The 369th was singled out for citations eleven times, and the entire regiment was awarded the Croix de Guerre for battlefield gallantry. Individually, 171 of its officers and enlisted men received the Croix de Guerre or the French Legion of Honor, although their own country didn't see fit to decorate any of them.

The 369th was demobilized on February 19, 1919, leaving a World War I service record that includes:

- The only volunteer regiment to serve during the war in France.
- The first regiment in U.S. history to serve as part of a foreign army.

- The first Allied regiment to reach the Rhine River.
- The longest combat service—191 days—of any American unit in World War I.
- The distinction of never losing a foot of ground, or losing a man by capture.
- The first combat regiment to arrive home after the armistice that ended the war.

The 369th Infantry Regiment was reorganized and recognized a part of the Army National Guard on September 26, 1924, and was known as the 369th until August 30, 1940, when it was converted to the 369th Coast Artillery, an antiaircraft unit. It was activated as part of the regular army on January 13, 1941, and transferred to various locations, including Los Angeles, California, before being sent to the Hawaiian island of Oahu in June 1942,where it participated in the defense of Pearl Harbor. Battery A, its searchlight unit, served on the nearby island of Maui.

The regiment was reorganized into the 369th Antiaircraft Battalion, the 870th Antiaircraft Automatic Weapons Battalion, and the 726th Searchlight Battery on December 12, 1943. The 870th and the 369th battalions were assigned to the Tenth Army on the island of Okinawa in 1944, and the 870th was detailed to combat duty in the nearby Kerama Retto Archipelago, where they relieved some of the troops of the 27th Division. One of its officers received a posthumous Distinguished Service Medal, and several officers and enlisted men earned the Bronze Star during the action that followed.

The original 369th Regiment was returned to New York in 1945. Although many of its men were discharged, many others stayed on active duty until they eventually retired.

Between September 11, 1950 and September 10, 1952, the 369th served in the Korean War as an antiaircraft battalion. Then it was reorganized as a transportation company and served in the Persian Gulf War.

Today it is known as the 369th Transportation Battalion of the Army National Guard, as well as the 15th Regiment of the New York Guard.

The unit reinforced its position as New York's own special heroes when it was assigned to the site of the World Trade Center after the twin towers were destroyed on September 11, 2001. Following regimental tradition, they were among the first National Guard outfits on the scene, and their trucks were on duty throughout the cleanup operations.

BIBLIOGRAPHY

Allen, Frederick Lewis. *Only Yesterday: An Informal History of the 1920s.* New York; NY: Harper & Row,1959.

Astor, Gerald. *The Right to Fight: A History of African-Americans in the Military.* Novato, CA: Presidio Press, 1998.

Buckley, Gail. *American Patriots.* New York: Random House, 2001.

Burton, Arthur T. *Black, Buckskin and Blue.* Austin, TX: Eakin Press, 1999.

Castle, Irene. *Castles in The Air.* Garden City NY: Doubleday, 1958.

Dalfiume, Richard M. *Desegregation of the U.S. Armed Forces: Fighting on Two Fronts: 1939–1953.* Columbia, MO: University of Missouri Press, 1969.

Edgerton, Robert B. *Hidden Heroism: Black Soldiers in America's Wars.* Boulder, CO: Westview Press, 2001.

Foner, Jack T. *Blacks and the Military in American History.* New York, NY: Praeger, 1974.

Holway, John B. *Red Tails, Black Wings: The Men of America's Black Air Force.* Las Cruces, NM: Yucca Tree Press, 1997.

Homan, Lynn M., and Reilly, Thomas. *Black Knights: The Story of the Tuskegee Airmen.* Gretna, LA: Pelican, 2001.

Johnson, James Weldon, *Black Manhattan.* New York: Athenaeum, 1972.

Katz, William Loren. *Eyewitness: The Negro in American History.* New York: Pitman Publishing, 1967.

Kenner, Charles T. *Buffalo Soldiers and Officers of the Ninth Cavalry.* Norman, OK: University of Oklahoma Press, 1999.

Lanning, Michael Lee. *The African-American Soldier.* New York: Carol Publishing Group, 1997.

Lewis, David Levering, *When Harlem Was in Vogue.* New York: Vintage Books, 1982.

Little, Arthur W. *From Harlem to the Rhine.* New York: Covici Friede, 1936.

McKay, Claude. *Negro Metropolis.* New York: Harcourt Brace Jovanovich, 1968.

Mershon, Sherie and Schlossman, Steven. *Foxholes and Color Lines.* Baltimore; Johns Hopkins University Press, 1998.

Osofsky, Gilbert. *Harlem: The Making of a Ghetto.* New York: Harper & Row, 1971.

Paradis, James M. *Strike the Blow for Freedom: The Sixth United States Colored Infantry in the Civil War.* Shippensburg, PA: White Mane Books, 1998.

Powell, Colin. *My American Journey.* New York: Random House, 1995.

Scott, Emmett. *Scott's Official History of the American Negro in the World War.* Chicago: Homewood Press, 1919.

Southern, Eileen. *Music of Black Americans.* New York: Norton, 1971.

Wascow, Arthur I. *From Race Riot to Sit-In: 1919 and the 1960s.* Garden City, NY: Anchor Books, 1960.

Williams, Charles Holston. *Negro Soldiers in World War I: The Human Side.* New York: AMS Press, 1979.

INDEX